THE BRUEN LOOP

THE BRUEN LOOP

THE JIMMY BRUEN STORY

GEORGE F. CROSBIE

IRISH AMERICAN BOOK COMPANY (IABC)
Boulder, Colorado

MERCIER PRESS
PO Box 5, 5 French Church Street, Cork
16 Hume Street, Dublin 2

Trade enquiries to CMD DISTRIBUTION,
55a Spruce Avenue, Stillorgan Industrial Park, Blackrock, Dublin

Published in the US and Canada by the
IRISH AMERICAN BOOK COMPANY
6309 Monarch Park Place, Niwot, Colorado, 80503
Tel: (303) 652 2710, (800) 452-7115
Fax: (303) 652 2689, (800) 401-9705

ISBN 1 85635 068 1

10 9 8 7 6 5 4 3 2 1

Printed in Ireland by Colour Books Ltd.

Contents

Foreword *by Peter Alliss*   7

Introduction   9

1   Small Jim   11

2   The Boys' Championship   14

3   1937 – A Great Year   18

4   1938 – A Golden Year   25

5   1938 – Walker Cup   32

6   Irish Close & British Open Championships 1938   42

7   An Irish Double   49

8   Amateur Championship 1939   56

9   69, 69 in the Open   63

10   66 on Newcastle   74

11   The War Years   79

12   Amateur Champion 1946   85

13   The Reluctant Hero   97

14   Walker Cup in America   107

15   1951 – Walker Cup   118

16   Bruen *v.* Carr   123

17   The Bruen Loop   130

18   Connie Griffin   137

19   Jimmy Bruen – The Man   143

Postcript – Recollections concerning Jimmy Bruen   150

FOREWORD

Peter Alliss

I was privileged to have a glimpse, albeit a brief one, of the magical skills of Jimmy Bruen. It was the early days of my national service and I was stationed at West Kirkby, not a million miles from the fabled links of Royal Liverpool and Birkdale, as it was known then. The Daily Telegraph Foursomes were being played and I, along with Guy Wolstenholme, managed to get along to watch Jimmy play with Wally Smithers at Formby.

Because of his amazing ball striking ability, allied to the most wondrous short game, anything from 100 yards from the flag usually produced a touch of magic. He had the most beautiful simple putting stroke, but then don't all good putters have that remarkable gift. All reports of his early days suggest that he had a great air of confidence bordering on arrogance and yet he managed to always show courtesy to an opponent, something that has almost disappeared in this hard world of commercialism.

Due to the war he, like many others, had his career curtailed and then shortly afterwards one of those silly accidents you can sometimes collect pottering about in the garden, started him on the road to retirement. Perhaps he did retire a little early but also he may have known that his amazing ability to recover from the worst of lies had gone. His injured wrists just wouldn't let him perform at the high standard to which he had become accustomed.

We played 18 holes together at Parkstone Golf Club where I was based as a professional. He was long past his competitive days, but his hair was still jet black, his swing lucid, perhaps not as violent as it was in days of yore, but the putting stroke was still silky and a delight to watch.

Through these pages many of you will be getting an insight into Jimmy Bruen for the first time. I know you'll enjoy reading about him because he was quite phenomenal.

Today we have Tiger Woods, years ago there was Vardon, Braid and Taylor, then Bobby Jones, Walter Hagen and Gene Sarazen, then in the late 1930s Snead, Hogan and, yes, Jimmy Bruen. Another world, agreed, but a giant talent the like of which only comes along perhaps once or twice every century.

INTRODUCTION

This book is more compiled than written. That it should be is no mere accident but an inevitability. Jimmy Bruen became an internationally known golfer when I was in my early teens. It was, therefore, impossible for me, or indeed any one person, to witness all the magnificent performances of this great player on the various golf courses where he achieved his fame.

There were, of course, thousands and thousands of witnesses but only the golf scribes recorded the facts. They painted the scenes and put their words in print. They too were in their thousands, famous, not so famous and many anonymous – they wrote for newspapers, magazines and radio. While some saw much of the great Bruen drama, others saw only the isolated event.

Even though all the information was there, it was spread out over so many different newspaper files – some – probably long gone – that it would have been a near impossible task to collect. Three dedicated people – Jimmy Bruen's father and mother, and later, Nell, his wife – collected the cuttings, photographs, letters, wires, score cards and even championship badges, and put them all in a large scrapbook.

Thanks to them, I have been able to look through the eyes of these journalists and witnesses, quoting where possible the name of the medium in which they wrote, to record – or perhaps the word is compile – the Jimmy Bruen Story.

There are so many sources and people I would like to thank that it would be impossible to name them all – but I am very grateful to them.

However, without the permission, help and encouragement of Mrs Nell Bruen and her son, Michael, this work would have been quite impossible. She talked to me many times about her husband. I hope that perhaps her satisfaction may rest in the fact that Jimmy's story has been told.

I have avoided using the word 'written' for I believe that no one could have written the Jimmy Bruen Story, with the exception of Jimmy himself – this he did on the golf course where, without a shadow of doubt, he played himself into the history of the game of golf.

I would particularly like to thank Peter Alliss for his Foreword – he has always been a great admirer of Jimmy Bruen.

Thanks are also due to Pat White of the *Examiner* for typing the original manuscript; to the *Examiner* photograpers, in particular Des Barry, for their help with the photographs; to the many writers, and newspapers, who wrote so enthusiastically about Jimmy and whom I quote; to the Directors of the *Examiner* for their sponsorship and the staff in Mercier Press who have been most encouringing and helpful at all times.

G F. CROSBIE
CORK

1

Small Jim

When a son was born to James and Margaret Bruen on 8 May 1920 in Belfast, little did they or anybody else know that a few days before his eighteenth birthday, the *Daily Telegraph* of London on its sports pages would carry the following headlines: 'Boy equals Bobby Jones' record'; 'Bruen greatest discovery of modern golf will be the youngest man ever to compete in Walker Cup match'. George Greenwood, the golfing correspondent of that newspaper, went on in his report to say:

> James Bruen, an Irish boy of seventeen from Cork, was the hero of the Walker Cup trial matches which were begun on the championship course here [St Andrew's] today. He accomplished an electrifying round of 68 which equals Bobby Jones' amateur record for the course and which is one stroke more than the professional record of 67, standing curiously enough in the name of another Irishman, W. Nolan of Portmarnock.
>
> Bruen is the greatest discovery of modern times in British Golf and his selection for the British team to meet America in the international match at St Andrew's next month is now an absolute certainty. No golfer of his age has ever played for either country. Even Bobby Jones was nineteen when he first came to England to play for America.

This boy, christened James O'Grady Bruen, was, in due course, to become the extraordinary and renowned golfer, Jimmy Bruen. His father, James J. Bruen, was a big man in every sense of the word. This ex-Connaught Ranger, with a gracious and gentle personality, stood well over 6 ft tall and was built accordingly. He was to be the major influence in his son's future as one of the world's greatest golfers.

James Bruen Snr hailed from Wilton in the city of Cork, in the south of Ireland, and at the time of his son's birth was working with the Munster and Leinster Bank in Belfast. Shortly afterwards the Bruen family returned to their native Cork.

Some years later, when Jimmy was about eleven years old, the Bruens set out on holiday to Rossapenna on the north coast.

They stopped on their way at a hotel in Bundoran, a seaside town where there is a fine golf course, and it so happened that Mrs Bruen became ill and had to retire to her bed. A doctor staying at the hotel, a Dr Cremin from Dublin, was called to attend her.

The following day, James Bruen Snr and Dr Cremin decided to play a game of golf. Cremin was a scratch golfer and Bruen Snr was around 6 handicap. It was arranged that 'small Jim' – as he was often called in those days, to distinguish him from his father – would go out on the course with Dr Cremin's young daughter, who was about the same age, and that the pair would play golf together with a cut down No. 5 to keep them amused. This apparently was the first time Jimmy Bruen ever played golf, and it is an interesting coincidence that the little girl who first played golf with him on the course at Bundoran was in later years to become his wife, Nell.

The Bruen family returned home to Cork and lost all contact with the Cremin family. Nell recalls that years later, when Jimmy was nineteen and already world-famous, she read his name in the headlines of the paper and asked her father could the boy be any relation of the Bruen family they had met in Bundoran. Jimmy happened to be playing at Portmarnock and Dr Cremin went out the next day and talked to Jimmy during a match, only to discover that, yes, indeed it was the same boy.

After the stay in Bundoran, James Bruen Snr had decided that his son was showing great talent for the game of golf, and when they got home he bought him a full set of cut-down clubs. From then on, young Jimmy spent many hours practising and playing in Cork Golf Club where he immediately came under the eye of Jack Higgins, the local professional. Jack was himself a very fine professional golfer who ought to have won at least one Irish Professional Championship, and was, in fact, runner-up to Fred Daly in 1940.

At this time Jimmy was a student in Presentation Brothers College, Cork, and in his spare time used to play rugby and hurling. It is pretty certain that the famous loop in young Jimmy's back swing came from his hurling days. What has now become known as the 'Bruen loop' is part and parcel of every hurler's method of striking the hurling ball. In fact, should you go to a hurling match you will see there thirty different versions of that famous 'Bruen loop'. During his school days, Bruen suffered an injury playing rugby and from then on gave up all sport in favour of golf.

In those years, Jack Higgins used to derive great amusement when visitors came to him looking for somebody with whom to play. Inevitably Jack would fix them up with this young boy who would emerge from the clubhouse wearing short trousers and a big smile on his rather round fat face. To the astonishment of the visitors, young Jimmy would play golf off a scratch handicap standard around the Cork Golf Club course – and inevitably win.

He played golf on every available occasion, and as soon as school was over would go straight down to the club. His father had a field at the back of their house and, for hours and hours until it was dark, young Jimmy used to hit golf balls there. He played a lot of his golf as well in the Muskerry Golf Club where he obtained his first handicap of 6, at the age of fifteen. A few weeks and several pieces of silverware later, he was down to scratch.

His enormous strength and his wonderful hands enabled him, even then, to swing a driver with devastating effect weighing a fraction under 15 ounces.

The first reference I can find in print to Jimmy Bruen was by an unknown correspondent, in May 1934, who wrote:

> A valued correspondent tells me that Master Bruen aged thirteen of that place of universal output, Cork, shapes like a golfing prodigy. His golf is long, accurate and well controlled. If he progresses as he is doing now he will be an amateur champion at an early age. It would be difficult for a good 8 handicap player to beat him today. We welcome Master Bruen heartily, in fact to tell the truth, we have been hoping for someone like him to appear. Provided his father restrains his efforts and makes him aim at well-controlled play, he may yet produce not a prodigy but what Ireland has long been due to give us, namely a real champion. We have, and have had, real champions but the modern generation has not supplied them so far.

The future would see that hope realised.

2

THE BOYS' CHAMPIONSHIP

The Boys' Championship always had a special place in Jimmy Bruen's heart. He first entered the Championship in 1935, at the age of fifteen, when it was played at Balgownie in Scotland. He was beaten in his second round by G. Roughead of Falkirk. The following year, in August, Jimmy travelled to Birkdale with his parents to have another go at this championship.

Earlier in the year, in June, young Jimmy had made his first real impact at home in the Irish Close Championship, held that year in Castlerock in Northern Ireland. His club handicap was now down to +1. To quote from a newspaper of the time:

> Visitors to the Co. Kerry resort, Parknasilla, had for some years back been returning with travellers' tales of an infant prodigy who performed golfing miracles on that little holiday course on the shores of Kenmare Bay. Cork itself occasionally served up stories of a school-boy golfer who was destined 'one day to make the tigers tremble'. Most Irish golfers were frankly sceptical and it was a sceptical crowd who followed Bruen on his first venture into serious golf at Castlerock in June. The event was the Irish Close Championship and the youthful Corkman confounded the critics and hammered his way into the quarter finals of his first senior [championship]. A record in itself no doubt and all the more amazing as Bruen had only recently passed his sixteenth birthday. John Burke barred his path to the semi-final. Burke won but the redoubtable John confessed after the game that he had 'taken no chances' and had been 'all out from start to finish'.

And so to Birkdale in August for the Boys' Championship before which he had just been delivered a new set of clubs made by Fred Smith of Dollymount Royal Dublin. Jimmy did a few days practice with these clubs on Birkdale and obviously found them satisfactory. During these practice days he also purchased a new putter from the professional in Birkdale. This was a Ben Sayers putter with a square handle, and it was the famous putter that James Bruen used virtually from then on. Although he did at times try other putters, he always came back to his favourite Ben Sayers which is now in Cork Golf Club.

Clearly, Jimmy took to Birkdale like a duck to water and went through to the final without very much trouble. In this final he met another sixteen-year-old, William Innes from Lanark in Scotland. Innes, head and shoulders taller than his opponent, was out-played with shots up to the hole and on the greens. Under a blazing sun, the two players, watched by their fathers, set out on a 36-hole final over the 6,700-yard course – the biggest test since the inception of this tournament in 1920. Innes fluffed his approach to lose the first hole. Bruen got down from 10 yards to become 2 up at the second. Following a good half in 4 at the third, the Irish boy became 3 up at the fourth by getting down from 4 feet. The fifth was halved in 4 and Bruen took the sixth to be 4 up by playing the better approach and he was down from 10 yards for a birdie 2 at the seventh for 5 up. Innes lost the eighth and, in trying to negotiate a stymie, he holed his opponent's ball. Bruen was giving a great display and a further win at the ninth made him 7 up and he was out in 35, 3 better than the scratch score. The figures for the first nine were: Bruen: 5, 4, 4, 3, 4, 5, 2, 4, 4, equalling 35; Innes: 6, 5, 4, 4, 4, 6, 3, 5, 6, equalling 43.

Bruen dropped from an unplayable lie for a penalty of one stroke at the tenth to take a 6 to lose that hole. After a half at the eleventh Bruen holed from 8 yards for a fantastic eagle 3 at the twelfth to be 7 up again. Innes got one back at the thirteenth by holing for a 2 to be 6 down, halving the fourteenth and fifteenth. Innes threw away a chance of reducing the arrears at the sixteenth by failing to hole from a yard for a win. Stymied again at the seventeenth, Innes failed to loft over his opponent's ball. Bruen took the eighteenth by holing a 5-yard putt to end the first round with a lead of seven holes. Scores inward half – Bruen: 6, 4, 3, 3, 5, 4, 5, 4, 4 for a total of 38, giving him a round of 73. Innes: 5, 4, 4, 2, 5, 4, 5, 4, 5 for a 38 giving him a total of 81.

In the second round, Bruen became 8 up by winning the second hole as a result of a perfect second shot. However, Innes got a hole back at the third where Bruen failed to negotiate his stymie. Innes was not putting well and when he failed from 2 feet at the fifth he became 8 down again. Bruen won also the short seventh in 3 to be 9 up. Bruen won the eighth to be 10 up and won the match at the next where he holed from 15 yards for his second eagle 3 of the day to finish off the match and become the Boys' Champion.

After the final, Jimmy was quoted as saying: 'I was beaten in the second round last year and then I became determined to win next time. My ambition is to become a senior champion and I have practised continuously to be a good golfer'.

In 1937, Jimmy won the Irish Close Championship and was chosen to play for Ireland in the home internationals in Portmarnock. Although again eligible to play in the Boys' Championship, he decided instead to practise for the internationals. He wrote to the secretary of the Boys' Championship, Major T. Scott:

> Nothing but the honour of playing for my country would keep me away from such a splendid championship but I must get some play in Dublin on Portmarnock links this week for the Internationals and Irish Open Amateur Championship. I thank the committee for the encouragement and kindness I got last year. I have much to thank you and the committee for – your guidance and encouragement. I am sure other boys will always look back as I do on your interest in us all as the finest headline we can get for our future guidance in sport.

In reply to his letter, Major Scott wrote:

> Thank you very much for your charming letter. It is now pinned on the notice board where it is being read with interest by the boys and others … You are of course quite right in not coming to Edinburgh and keeping yourself for the Internationals, but we are all sorry not to have you with us. It was nice of you to speak with affection of the Boys' Championship. I have received many such expressions in the past, there is an atmosphere that does not exist at any other meeting, and it is sad when boys pass on to be seen no more with us. Carry on the tradition of the Boys' Championship, Jimmy, accept your success with modesty and take your whackings like a man. Goodbye, Jimmy, and the best of luck from us all.

In 1939, when on holidays in Carnoustie, Jimmy went along to watch the Boys' Championship again, and in particular to support a small group of his Irish friends taking part. There is no doubt that he was a welcome VIP on that occasion. Unfortunately, his Irish colleagues were not as successful as Jimmy had been himself.

Jimmy's interest in young players was evident at this early

stage and remained with him all his life. No young player who consulted him or sought advice ever met with anything but the greatest kindness and all the help Bruen could give.

3

1937 – A Great Year

1937, 1938 and 1939 were to be probably the three most out-standing years in the career of Jimmy Bruen. Certainly they were to be his busiest years.

The Cork Scratch Cup, played in Cork Golf Club at Easter every year, is, along with the West of Ireland Championship, played in Rosses Point, a useful 'pipe-opener' to the golfing season in Ireland. In the field in 1937 there were such notable players as internationals Dr J. D. MacCormack, J. C. Browne, Dr William O'Sullivan, Redmond Simcox, and of course, young Jimmy Bruen. Bruen won his way to the final without the slightest trouble and played Redmond Simcox whom he beat by 7 and 6 in a 36-hole final. The winning margin of 7 and 6 was far from flattering to Simcox, who did not experience the best of luck around the greens, and this, coupled with spells of brilliance on the part of Bruen, was the deciding factor.

In May, Jimmy went to Sandwich to play in the St George's Vase, which was then a 36-hole stroke competition. With scores of 73 and 74 he finished second, three shots behind D. H. R. Martin of Royal St George's. *The Sporting News* reported:

> Bruen returned (second round) 74 for a total of 147. It was a magnificent feat for one so young. Bruen is the reigning Boys' champion and clearly a golfer of the highest promise. He is of a good shape for the game, not too tall and very strongly built. His swing is not at first sight prepossessing for there is a suspicion of a lift and shrugging movement of the shoulders but he comes through with a fine freedom. He hits very hard and he also goes very straight. Doubtless we shall see more of him in the next few days, but at any rate, handsome is as handsome does. Nobody but a really good golfer could have done such a score and his fellow Irishmen who ought to know him think almost unutterable things of him. His round was the more meritorious in that he missed great scoring chances by taking 4s at the three obvious places for 3s – namely the Maiden, Hades and the sixteenth.

Two days later, most of the players went to Deal for the Prince of

Wales Cup. Here again James Bruen had two 75s in bad weather conditions to finish second to Charlie Stowe's two 74s. To quote the *Sporting News* again:

> They found the course in capital order and considerably drier than its neighbour but rendered formidable by a fierce southerly wind and squalls of rain … In the circumstances there were some very good scores in the morning, and, in particular, the three 75s of Micklem, Levinson and Bruen. Probably the best of the three rounds was Bruen's for he had the worst of the wind and rain. He played with the same confidence as at Sandwich though he had never seen the course before … With something of a lifting and a sway he gave the ball a notable wallop – it is the best word I can think of – he keeps very straight and is a beautifully smooth and bold putter. When he puts the ball in he takes it as a matter of course, and when he just fails from 10 yards or so, he appears rather surprised and annoyed … he played magnificently and ended with six 4s in a row. Only those who know Deal in this particular wind can fully appreciate this feat. It is of no use to argue about such a golfer, one can only salute him.
>
> [Stowe] was the only man who humanly speaking could catch Bruen … All sympathy is due to Bruen and all praise to his conqueror.

We have two inter-club national competitions in Ireland, the Senior Cup and the Barton Shield, and, in due course, Jimmy was to assist in bringing both titles to Cork Golf Club. The Senior Cup is a team of five playing singles, and the Barton Shield is a foursome competition with two pairs making up a team. At the end of the round in the Barton Shield, the total holes up in both matches is what determines the winners. In 1937, Cork Golf Club, led by young Jimmy Bruen, won the Barton Shield. This was played as a pipe-opener to the Irish Close Championship, held that year in Ballybunion in the month of June. It is interesting to read the press report of that final:

> For the first time since the inception of the competition, Cork Golf Club won the Barton Shield at Ballybunion, the beaten finalists were Portmarnock but it was a desperately close affair and the Dubliners only admitted defeat after two extra holes had been played in the second match. [In the case of a tie in this competition the second pair play the tie holes and whoever wins a hole first decides the competition.] The hero of the affair was James Bruen, Boys' Champion, who did yeoman service for Cork and in the

nerve-racking finish produced shot after shot which only a champion could produce. Partnered by K. John [Dr John Kiely a leading Cork surgeon and father of Dave Kiely an Irish rugby international and later a leading Munster golfer] who was the acme of imperturbable steadiness, Bruen played one of his best games and Cork may well thank him for bringing home the shield to Little Island for the first time.

The final result was: – G. Crosbie (my father) and S. McCarthy lost to J. D. MacCormack and J. A. Healy by one hole. J. Bruen and K. John beat C. A. Carroll and J. Owens by two holes. It is interesting to note too that the Portmarnock team of those days consisted of two internationals, Dr J. D. MacCormack and Charlie Carroll. There were no internationals on the Cork team because at this stage James Bruen had not yet been selected for Ireland, but his obvious brilliance was an inspiration to his club.

On the next few days over the famous Ballybunion golf course – probably one of the best golf courses in Ireland and the British Isles, if not the world, the Irish Championship took place. Young Bruen battled his way without any great difficulty into the final, and so also did the leading Irish amateur of those days, the famous John Burke. John Burke at this stage was a Walker Cup player, Irish international, and also he had made the south of Ireland championship almost his own. He was unquestionably the leading amateur golfer in Ireland. They had met in the last eight of this championship in the previous year, and of course the experience of Burke beat the sixteen-year-old Bruen. Everybody was looking forward to the clash of these two wonderful players.

Bruen won the match by 3 and 2 and became the youngest player ever to win the Irish Close Championship. One newspaper reported:

> Never was victory more merited than was Bruen's and the match ended on the thirty-fourth green with a 3 and 2 victory, hundreds of spectators who had perforce to suppress their excitement all through the match let themselves go in prolonged outburst of applause for the victor. Yesterday's final will rank as one of the best ever played in the Championship.

The quality of the golf in what is regarded as one of the most testing courses in the country may best be gauged from the figures.

These show that for the thirty-two holes Bruen played in only two over 4s. One thing, and one alone, decided the issue – that was Bruen's deadly accuracy on the greens. Not once in the course of the day did he make a semblance of a mistake.

In the morning round of the 36-hole final Bruen led by three holes going to the sixteenth but unaccountably lost all the last three holes to get to the halfway stage all square. In the afternoon Bruen won four of the first five holes to be 4 up and, though his lead was reduced to 1 after thirty-two holes, he went on to win the next two holes for the match 3 and 2. This was to be his first victory in senior golf but there were of course many more victories to follow.

Many years afterwards my father used to tell a very nice story about this final. Dr J. D. MacCormack – himself many times winner of the Irish Championship and a leading Irish golfer at the time – was, like many others, somewhat sceptical about this young prodigy Bruen, and had not seen him in action until they arrived for the Ballybunion championship. Apparently, J. D., as he was usually called in Ireland, followed every shot of Bruen all day with increasing amazement, and at the twenty-seventh hole in the afternoon – which was a short pitch hole – Bruen apparently missed the green and left himself with a very awkward chip indeed, downhill on very bare seaside ground and the green falling away from him. J. D. turned to my father and said, 'Now this will test the young fellow', whereupon young Jimmy, without the least hesitation, played the most beautiful 'cut up' pitch stone dead, after which J. D.'s only remark was, 'Be japers I've seen everything now'.

In July, Jimmy Bruen went to Portrush to play in the Irish Open Championship which was won by Bert Gadd. Jimmy finished joint sixth and leading Irish player – pro or amateur – and, of course, he won the best amateur prize. The *Cork Examiner* of 30 July reported:

> The hero of an exciting day was James Bruen, Jr, the seventeen-year-old Cork golfer who holds the Boys' Championship and the major Irish amateur title. Though suffering from tonsillitis and advised by his doctor to withdraw, Bruen insisted on completing the championship and had the remarkably low aggregate of 292, the best amateur performance. Bruen's first round yesterday, a 72, created a new amateur course record and later he beat this with a mag-

nificent 71. Although during the interval he had debated whether having a temperature he should retire, Bruen played perfect golf.

Another report in that newspaper names the team to represent Ireland in the Amateur International matches at Portmarnock in the first three days of September: J. C. Brown, Waterford, J. Bruen, Muskerry, J. Burke, Lahinch, C. Ewing, Co. Sligo, J. A. Flaherty, Langley Park, L. O. Munn, North West, J. D. MacCormack, Grange, R. M. McConnell, Royal Portrush, W. M. O'Sullivan, Dooks, G. F. Owens, Skerries. Reserves: W. J. Gill, Portmarnock and J. R. Carr, Royal Co. Down.

The first two days obviously did not go well for Ireland when they were beaten both by England and Scotland. Jimmy Bruen did not really come into his own until the final day against Wales when Ireland was struggling to avoid the wooden spoon. Partnering L. O. Munn, he beat D. H. Lewis and R. M. D. Lloyd by one hole in the foursomes, and in the singles he demolished the Welsh champion by 5 and 4. Quoting from the *Irish Press* of 4 September:

> Jimmy Bruen more than vindicated himself in his match against the Welsh champion, Lewis, and played the best golf seen during the tournament to win by 5 and 4. He was dormie 6 having shot the first twelve holes in three under 4s – amazing figures considering the length of the course and the very strong wind. He slipped up for the first time at the long thirteenth where he took 6, but he settled the matter on the fourteenth where he was conceded a putt for yet another 3 in the match.

Later on in September of that year, Jimmy added another course record to the list. Playing at Muskerry Golf Club, Cork, in the Mackesy Cup, which is an 18-hole stroke competition, he had an amazing round of 65. The *Cork Examiner* reported:

> James Bruen, Jr, the Irish champion created a new course record of 65. The previous record of 66 was held by Dr W. M. O'Sullivan (Dooks). Bruen played magnificent golf, his card including six birdies and one eagle. Altogether he had nine 3s. His performance was all the more meritorious because of the fact that conditions were far from easy with a strong wind and occasionally heavy showers sweeping across the course.

Par for the course at Muskerry is 72 and Bruen's card read as follows: 5, 3, 4, 4, 4, 3, 3, 3, 5 = 34 for the first nine, 3, 3, 4, 4, 4, 4, 3, 3, 3 = 31 for the second nine, giving a total of 65. It is interesting to note that playing off +2 he returned a 67 which was only beaten by one other card – a 65 – on the day.

Also in that month there is a nice tail piece. In a report in the *Daily Mail* about Bobbie Locke (in those days the South African Amateur star) and Jim Ferrier (the Australian Amateur star who that year had been runner-up to Hector Thompson in the British Amateur Championship at St Andrew's), Jeffrey Simpson wrote:

> Dominion golfers claim that Locke and Ferrier are the world's outstanding amateur golfers. Many will dispute that. Locke has always found someone too good for him here and I fancy the seventeen-year-old Irish boy, James Bruen, younger by two years, would give him a fight any time.

In the next two years, the brilliant Jimmy Bruen was to pit himself against the world's best players, both professional and amateur.

In October 1937, Henry Cotton, then the British Open Golf champion wrote in a review of the golf scene:

> There is little doubt that British amateur golf is in low water. An American holds our championship, and from what I have heard of the recent play in the Internationals at Portmarnock few newcomers of any striking ability have been produced by the four home countries. One of the exceptions is James Bruen Jr, the Cork youngster who will not be eighteen until next May, yet who holds the native championship of Ireland and therefore ranks as the best golfer in that country. Bruen touched brilliance in his match against David Lewis, the new Welsh champion, and there is no doubt that he will be one of the first choices for Britain's Walker Cup team. If he is selected he will beat John Langley's record of being the youngest British international.
>
> Langley is one of my pupils and I would like to give some advice to Bruen. I saw Bruen play at Sandwich in the British Amateur Championship. He is determined to attack the ball but I should like to see him develop a smoother swing. If he is wise, Bruen will concentrate on cultivating an easier style. One encouraging feature of his play in my opinion is his capacity for hard work, but he will be well advised not to overdo it.

This was the first time that Henry Cotton saw Jimmy Bruen play.

I think he might subsequently have modified his views on Bruen's swing.

4

1938 – A Golden Year

In May 1938, twenty-four players were selected by the Walker Cup selectors for trials in St Andrew's where the Walker Cup was to take place some weeks later. Three Irish players were selected and they were James Bruen, Cecil Ewing and Johnny Fitzsimons of Royal Portrush. In the practice rounds for these trials Jimmy started to cause a sensation. He started off never having seen the course before to go around in 71 twice. The *Cork Examiner* reporter wrote:

> I had a word with Bruen when he had finished and he told me he had never felt better and was playing at the peak of his game. He told me he had had trouble with his caddies over the size of his bag. He had nineteen clubs when he came to St Andrew's. [This was, of course, before the fourteen-club rule came into being.] This is the first time he has been here and he realises that the vast putting greens with their hillocks round and about require a special putter so Bruen bought one of the wooden putters much in favour amongst the local players. The caddies thought that his bag was too big and each time he has had a new caddy. The St Andrew's course is dry and hard and the players are driving enormous distances. At the twelfth hole Bruen had actually to play back so far was his tee shot.

The next day the trials proper began and the twenty-four players went out in groups of three. Jimmy Bruen was playing against the English player, J. E. Gent, and the Scottish player, A. E. Dowie. The description in the *Cork Examiner* of 6 May 1938 is worth quoting:

> When Jimmy Bruen was reeling off his marvellous rounds during the days he was getting acquainted with the strange holes, those little humps and hollows which guard the spacious greens of old St Andrew's and getting to know where the multitudes of bunkers were hidden from the green. People said 'Oh, this is only practice?' Today in the two rounds of the actual trials the Cork lad played dazzling golf.
>
> He drew the onlookers who crowded after him leaving the other players to themselves, watching the marvellous shots ...

Bruen played with a quiet calm and assurance which showed that
even in the greatest strain he is not likely to be perturbed. He made
his place on the team an absolute certainty. He was by far and away
the most brilliant performer.

In his first round Bruen did a 68 which equalled the amateur record of St Andrew's achieved by Bobby Jones when he won his
first Open Championship in 1927, and it is one stroke less than
Dublin professional Willie Nolan's record made in 1935.

Bruen had many sensational holes but the most remarkable
was the long fifth in the morning, reaching the green with a drive
and a No. 3 and holing a long putt for an eagle 3. He then took
the four holes from the eighth to the eleventh each in 3s. At the
dreaded road hole, most famous in the world, he holed a long
putt over the shoulder of a bunker to get another eagle 3. In his
second round, Bruen went out in the marvellous figures of 33 but
on the last nine holes his putts would not drop and he took 38 to
finish in 71.

The purpose of the tests was to assist the selectors in choos-
ing the ten best players in Great Britain and Ireland to meet the
United States on 3 and 4 June. The form of Bruen gave complete
satisfaction.

Playing with the greatest equanimity and hitting the ball
prodigious distances – his tee shots were always ahead of his
rivals – Bruen had many remarkable holes. His figures for his
first run are worth quoting: Out – Par 4, 4, 4, 4, 5, 4, 4, 3, 4 = 36;
Bruen – 4, 4, 4, 5, 3, 4, 4, 3, 3 = 34; In – Par 4, 3, 4, 4, 5, 4, 4, 5, 4 =
37 for a total of 73; Bruen – 3, 3, 5, 3, 5, 4, 4, 3, 4 = 34 for a total of
68.

On the same day, George Greenwood in the *Daily Telegraph*
wrote:

> Bruen is as much a golfing genius as Jones or Henry Cotton, and it
> would not be surprising if the Irish youth in his quest for fame
> achieved a similar measure of success. In the matter of style and
> method there is little in common between Bruen and either of these
> two distinguished players. Standing rather wide with the ball al-
> most opposite his left foot Bruen takes his hands back unusually
> high where at the top of the swing there is a slight suspicion of a
> waving of the club head.
>   Obviously he is gathering power for the down swing and the

subsequent blow is terrific. He uses a deep face driver weighing nearly fifteen ounces and tees the ball very high ...

... For the past twenty years I have seen the world's greatest golfers attack the old course at St Andrew's but none has ever made the task look so supremely easy as Bruen who, with the exception of the fifth and fourteenth holes never took a club stronger than a mashie for a second shot ...

Playing with such superb confidence and hitting the second shots so accurately there seemed no reason why Bruen should not get a 3 at every hole. There should have been six of them in a row but for a slip at the twelfth. Bruen went boldly for a putt of 7 yards, ran 4 feet past and missed his return. The only mistake in an otherwise glorious round.

The following day, Bruen, playing against Gordon Peters in the singles match over thirty-six holes, went around in 71 and 73 and beat his Walker Cup companion by seven holes. The newspaper headlines said it all: 'Cork Boy's amazing display in Walker Cup trials at St Andrew's'; 'Bruen equals Bobby Jones' record'; 'Sensational driving and putting, dazzling golf in difficulties – Regarded as a certainty for the team'; 'Bruen smashing round of 68'; 'Boy equals Bobby Jones' record'; 'Bruen greatest discovery of modern golf'; 'A new Bobby Jones from Ireland'; 'Baby of Walker Cup trials equals Bobby Jones' record'.

At the end of the trials, Henry Cotton, writing about the team now selected and including Jimmy Bruen, wrote:

... the scores produced were good enough to win an Open Championship. Fancy an eighteen-year-old boy, James Bruen, doing 282 in four rounds – amazing ... here was a mere boy playing it [St Andrew's] with a wise head and a technique that left everybody gasping. I have not known a player do such scores no matter what his age. Bruen has indeed set a standard for all golfers ... The praise given to young Bruen has been more than deserved and he must be counted on to give us at least one point during the big days against the Americans in June ... Jim is a heavily built, dark-haired youngster with small penetrating eyes. Unusually level-headed for his age but still a modest boy at heart. He wields a heavy full length deep-faced driver of 15 ounces and hits the ball with all his might as far as anybody. He employs a wide, very pigeon-toed stance, swings his hands high and hits the ball with a crack like a whip. He plays his iron shots as crisply and with as much assurance as any professional. His swing is not elegant and although he appears to lunge at the ball a more observant eye will see that his left side is as solid as a rock at impact.

The secret of his game appears to me to be in his large strong hands. They hold the club as firm as any player I know. This allows him to be sure of a solid square club face at impact ... he can play all the shots, runups, pitches, half shots and forcing ones. How far this lad will go I will not venture to state, surely he must be one of the world's greatest players before many years have passed. I base this not so much on his remarkable scores or on his swing, but on his golfing brain and his temperament.

P. B. Lucas, himself later to be a Walker Cup player and captain, wrote the following:

James (small Jim) Bruen ... is eighteen today and the talk of the golfing world. In all these years of going the rounds of tournaments ... I never saw a player so clearly stamped with class at so early an age as this young scion of an Irish family in Cork. Looking out of the Grand Hotel across the eighteenth fairway on the old course at St Andrew's, James Bruen, golf's ambitious young history-maker told me something about himself and his ideas for the future. 'I started to play golf in Cork when I was about 12 ... I did not have any lessons but started in to learn the game myself rather than have people tell me what to do or what not to do. At school I did not play a lot of golf ... I don't drink or smoke in the ordinary way although if I do well in a tournament, maybe I will have a glass or two of champagne ... I play off a handicap of +4 at home ... I have had a 64 at Cork Golf Club and 65 at Muskerry which are my best rounds ... I would not turn professional unless I thought it would be worth my while to do so, and I'd have to win an open championship before that. What I think of mainly when I am playing or practising is my left hand. When I am using that hand well I can be pretty sure that my game will be fairly good, but as soon as I start getting my left hand too much over the shaft, I'm pulling it in instead of letting it go out after the ball, I know I will be wrong. I am going to concentrate on the Walker Cup match here in June and shall not be competing in the Amateur Championship in Troon. If I did well in this I would be dead tired for the Walker Cup match which comes on immediately after the Championship.

'... what is the good of playing for your country if you do not give yourself up to do all you can to reach your peak when the match comes along? ...'

'You came in for some cruel criticism in the championship last year in Sandwich,' I said, 'how did you feel about it? We never had your story of the case.' 'It was very hard at the time ... because I can honestly say that it was not my fault ... What happened was this, at the fourteenth at Sandwich my opponent hooked away to the left in the rough into a little ditch. I saw him beginning to roll up his trousers and he asked me to go over and have a look at his ball to see how it was lying. He asked me if I thought it was casual water and naturally I said I did not think it was. Then I asked someone if there was any member of the Championship committee about who could give us a ruling. His caddy then turned to me and said, "If you don't know the rules any better than that, you had better take the next boat back to Ireland". I just told my opponent to go ahead and do what he liked about the ball.

'Next day the papers at home came out with great headlines "Cork Boy in unpleasant incident at Sandwich".

'If I had asked for it I would not have minded, but to be criticised when you have done nothing to deserve it breaks your heart for a while'. And that is why I think this boy is going to be one of the greatest players of all time – because he has the courage to fight against these things. They tried to break his heart last year but all Bruen did was to go home and win his native championship.

Another newspaper cutting of the day has one nice little heading: 'Appointed yesterday a member of the team to represent Great Britain against the United States in the Walker Cup Golf Contest, James Bruen, today celebrates his eighteenth birthday and tomorrow – goes back to school in Presentation College, Cork'.

Before the Walker Cup, the *Evening Gazette* of Friday, 3 June, published in a series called 'Open Letters to the Famous', 'No. 2 to Mr James Bruen, Walker Cup Wonder' written by J. L. Hodson. The heading reads 'Your Success is Important'.

Dear Mr Bruen,
I don't suppose you have any notion how much pleasure your round of 68 at St Andrew's when you equalled Bobby Jones' record, gave to golfers like me. And not only golfers, you're only eighteen and you are 'hitting them out of sight'. I hope you'll keep on doing it. I hope you'll win your Walker Cup match, but if you don't, well, you'll win next time ... a lot of first class men have their ups and downs ...

It's the sticking-to-it quality that matters. You have got that I imagine. Golf is a very searching game; it finds out the weak spots. There is a lot of time to think and get upset between one shot and

the next ... It doesn't as a rule become any easier as you get older
... I am told you started playing golf because an injury at rugby
kept you out of the team. In other words you turned misfortune
into profit – a knack that good men have ...

I was particularly glad to see you being picked for the Walker
Cup team because I think, we as a nation, ought to be rather more
alert in spotting youth and giving it a chance ...

It is a curious thing that as our youngsters have grown, on the
average heavier and bigger ... they have grown rather more boyish. That's due to the fact I suppose that they go to school rather
longer and more and more of them go on to the universities. Doing
that keeps them young, makes them in the long run healthier and
stronger and extends age at the far end. On the other hand they are
free for a longer time from having to make decisions. I find a lot of
boys of seventeen and eighteen who ... are just drifting along ...
When a man doesn't know which target he is aiming at, he isn't
very likely to hit the bull, is he?

I dare say you know so far as golf goes what you are aiming at
... Probably you won't remember and possibly not have heard of
Captain Albert Ball, V. C. the Nottingham boy ... commissioned at
eighteen and given the freedom of his native city when he was
twenty-one because of his exploits in the air ...

I have said in one of my other open letters that we need Nelsons of the air today. Ball was one of them 'a short little chap with
longish black hair and eyes like a hawk'. How monstrous and tragic it is that he should have been killed. I have no doubt at all that
British youth will, if the lamentable need arises, provide all ... the
Nelsons ... we want. The right stuff thrives on responsibility as the
last war shows ... I can't tell you how much I hope your generation
will not have to go through all that again ...

My generation ... have done a lot of bungling. But I think we
stand a very good chance of avoiding war if we convince the dic-
tators that we are as tough and tenacious and determined as ever
we were. That is another reason why I am glad you are on the
Walker Cup team. Somebody ought to send Hitler a postcard about
you.

... I was struck by reading that your staunchest supporter is
your mother ... Was there ever a remarkable man who didn't have
a remarkable mother? ... The modern fashion is to let children go
their own way ... But most of us require a certain amount of disci-
pline ... But a lad who brings himself up, makes his own decisions,
puts his own curb on himself – he will probably turn out better still.
There is no royal road for youth – no way that's invariably right.

Just as there is none for the right age to marry ... But just as men seem to be boyish for a longer period nowadays, so they put off marriage to a later date. If it helps them to know their own minds more surely then it is all to the good. I hope Mr Bruen that you will be as successful in your job at earning a living as you are in your golf – I dare say you will. The same quality will tell and I hope that what you have done will inspire British youth generally to get his teeth into whatever he is tackling. If there is any way of winning that's it. Good luck in today's match.

Yours sincerely,

J. L. Hodson.

5

1938 – WALKER CUP

Before the start of the 1938 Walker Cup there was tremendous speculation as to whether the young wonder boy, Jimmy Bruen, should play number one in the singles. At the time, the great American player, Johnny Goodman, was the reigning American Amateur champion, having already won the Open Championship of America in 1933. Many people looked forward to a clash between these two good players. There was much speculation too as to whether Bruen was too young to lead the Walker Cup side. That John Beck, the captain of the British side, did play him in that position, is now history. However, Bruen did not play Goodman as, the previous week, Charlie Yates had won the British Amateur Championship beating Cecil Ewing in the final. Hence, Yates was promoted to number one in the American team.

Bruen continued to play fantastic golf around St Andrew's in the practice rounds. He was so keen to play a match with Henry Cotton, with whom he hadn't played, that he asked John Beck, his captain, if he could do so. Cotton was there as a sort of unofficial adviser to the Walker Cup team. Beck had his reservations as he thought it might put Bruen off, but Bruen was quite insistent and, in due course, they did play a practice round together. Once again young Bruen went round St Andrew's in 69 shots, the same score as Henry Cotton, and the fact that he was playing with a great man made absolutely no difference to Jimmy.

The great day dawned and in the first foursome Jimmy Bruen and H. G. Bentley of Hesketh were the first foursomes pair to start. F. J. C. Pignon of the *Daily Mail* takes up the story:

> There were signs early today that the British players were inclined to suffer from that malignant complaint – 'nerves' or 'inferiority complex' more aptly described by golfers as an attack of the 'jitters'.
>
> But as the day progressed the home golfers played like heroes. Even in the one match which Britain lost, the will to win was evident ...
>
> But there is another story which all St Andrew's will be telling

for many a day.

It is about James Bruen, the eighteen-year-old Cork schoolboy, the youngest member of the team and Harry Bentley ... who carried the millstone of a deficit all day.

They fought back to all square and almost won the last hole with 10,000 cheering spectators, including the Duke of Kent ... watching them. Never have I seen a greater match. The British pair were opposed to Johnny Fischer, former American champion, and Charles Kocsis, one of the best short game players in America.

Bruen, apparently for the first time in his life, suffered the agony of playing before a big crowd on a great occasion. He did not play like the destroying giant we had seen in the practice games. He did not play badly but he gave his partner plenty to do because the Americans were longer and straighter. Three times the home players held the lead and each time they went shooting back to all square before they reached the ninth level.

What appeared to have settled the issue was the fact that Kocsis and Fischer, approaching and putting beautifully, had five of the six holes from the eighth to the thirteenth in 3 each. They actually lost one of these at the eleventh – where Bruen holed a long curling putt for a 2 but they were 2 up on the balance.

From that moment, Bruen and Bentley fought gallantly against their defeat. They were robbed of the seventeenth hole where Bruen played one of the best shots of the match to reach this treacherous green. Kocsis was bunkered in what is regarded as an almost impossible place, corner of the green, but Fischer left the recovery dead.

When Bentley left his second to the eighteenth short in that little dip which is called the 'Valley of Sin', the crowd moaned for Britain had lost another hole, and the leading partnership went into lunch with the uncomfortable feeling of a three hole deficit.

The Americans had the homeward half in 33 and went round in 72 and the home players' in par 75.

Try as they might Bentley and Bruen, who had now settled down in a fine combination, could not make any impression ... America were still 3 up until they lost the ninth to a birdie 3. That began Britain's recovery. Bruen holed a 10-foot putt for a second 2 of the day at the eleventh hole and they were only 1 down.

... At the seventeenth Bruen played a glorious brassy to the green. Kocsis tried to match it, but his ball ran over the green and he was on the road ... Bentley, with that rusty old putter of his, holed from 20 yards for a birdie 3. The British pair almost embraced in their joy while the crowd cheered them. It seemed a pity that they could not have won the match after this, but Bruen, now playing like the great golfer we have seen in practice, could be forgiven for failing to hole from 12 yards although the Americans had to hole from 4 feet to halve the match. The British pair had the last nine holes in 32 and went round in 68. The Americans too beat par by four strokes ...

There is a nice little story written many years later by Leonard Crawley, after Jimmy had died. In describing this foursomes match against the Americans, Leonard wrote:

> Having been at one time a long way down and almost a lost cause Bruen had a putt of 20 feet across that innocent looking treacherous slope on the last green to win the match. One may well imagine Bentley's feelings, having nursed his youthful sick partner through a long day and desperately important match, when he heard him whisper, 'Harry I think I can hole it'. His reply was firm and imme- diate: 'No, you can't, put booger dead', and he did.

After that magnificent halved match of Bentley and Bruen along with the excellent wins of Gordon Peters and Hector Thompson and of Leonard Crawley and Frank Pennink, Britain led by that valuable one point after the day's foursomes. And so to the sin- gles next day. No better description of that match can I find than that of P. B. (Laddie) Lucas writing in the *Sunday Express*:

> The match everyone wanted to see in the morning was of course that between the new British Amateur champion, Charles Yates, and James Bruen, who has rightly been heralded as the new white hope of amateur golf today.
> And what a game it was. Right from the start Bruen went at his man hammer and tongs, matching him shot for shot. He never seemed to be in the least bit worried by the reputation that his ad- versary had achieved since he landed in this country one month ago. Of the two I thought Yates to be the steadier. He looked to me to be more likely to go on doing fours all the time and just waiting for Bruen to slip up. You have no doubt heard a certain amount about the so-called kink in Bruen's swing. In point of fact if you stand directly behind the line of play you will see that he starts the back swing very much on the inside arc and then as he gets to the top he lifts his hands forward a shade so that when the swing begins he is really hitting straight forward along the lineup to the hole. All the accurate hitters have this straight attack on the ball. The first two holes were halved in 4 a piece with Bruen playing a first rate recovery from a bunker at the back of the second green.

The ball when it pitched actually came back a foot and then down went a good solid 9-footer to give him a thoroughly heartening start. Away he went like one brim full of confidence … And so it went on, the American with his 4s and 3s was sitting back waiting for his opponent to crack … The perfectly ordinary half in 3 at the short eighth and another half at the ninth meant that Bruen was out in 34 and 1 down, almost without noticing it, to Yates' 33. Well there is a limit to everything and when the American did make his first mistake, three putts on the thirteenth green, Bruen let his chance slip and missed a tiny one to square the match. He did the same again at the very next hole to become 2 down and with Yates playing the home hole quite perfectly with a drive, chip and a putt – how well he let his putter follow the ball without giving the first sign of a jerk – Bruen finished the round 3 down.

Bruen hadn't taken his chances and he didn't seem to be quite the attacking force that he was in his foursome with Bentley on Friday afternoon. In the afternoon Bruen put up a great fight, through the outward half he kept plodding along and by the ninth he had got one hole back from Yates only to see the good work cancelled out again at the tenth, but even so he was not done yet, for the third time in two days he got a 2 at the short eleventh and then just when we thought that perhaps he might make a great comeback he missed oh such a small putt on the fifteenth green as he had done in the morning. It was obvious then that nothing short of a miracle would make up for this lapse.

Although Bruen lost that match against probably one of the best amateurs in the world at the time, he still seemed to inspire the rest of the team who duly won sufficient singles for Britain to win the Walker Cup for the first time. I think it is correct to say that most players and most commentators of the time gave the inspiration of Bruen as the main reason for the British side's success. There were, of course, other reasons but the young Irish boy seemed to electrify the whole team. An article in the *Cork Examiner* of Friday, 10 June 1938 gives an accurate and fair assessment of Bruen's contribution to this win. Written by an eye-witness, the article headed 'Reflections on the Walker Cup' is, I think, well worth quoting:

> Having witnessed the excitement bordering on hysteria that reigned at St Andrew's on Friday and Saturday of last week when a British team won the Walker Cup for the first time, I am making an effort to collect my thoughts sufficiently to give an impression of

the part played by the Irish representatives who were included in the British team.

If any of my readers have had the experience of trying to keep track of eight 36-hole matches – all of equal importance – on a course where many of the holes are so alike that it is easy to get them mixed up in one's mind, they would have some idea of the difficulty of my task. The thought that is innermost in my mind is – how can sixteen human beings maintain such an incredibly high standard of golf under the conditions that prevailed? In the first place, those who have only had experience of golf – even championship golf as we know it – in this country (Ireland) will find it difficult to visualise a crowd varying according to circumstances from 3,000 to 10,000 people watching one match.

On every occasion, immediately the drives were struck there was a wild rush to get into position of vantage to see one of the second shots played. From there to the green the same thing occurred. This rush has to be heard to be believed. It can be very fairly compared to the thunder of a cattle stampede before a prairie fire. This, combined with the natural strain of the occasion plus the inclemency of the weather, provided as severe a test of golfing nerves as can be conceived.

With regard to the weather, while the wind might have been stronger it was strong enough to make things difficult, but the most unsettling factor was provided by the intermittent showers of rain which kept continually altering the speed of the enormous greens – some of which measure up to 150 yards in length – and which must have rendered putting under the circumstances almost a nightmare. The terrific strain must have been hardest on the youngest player, namely James Bruen. Most of those competing and especially those of the US team had considerable experience of playing under such trying circumstances. Furthermore, the manner in which the young Cork player had been 'written-up' by certain sections of the press did not help to lighten his burden … I can only find one word to describe how 'young Jimmy' faced up to the situation and that is 'magnificent'….

The article continues:

All things considered, Bruen came through his first really big event with flying colours and he showed 15,000 people that, despite his youth and the run of luck rather against him, he can fight an uphill battle against the relentless and redoubtable opponent to the very last ditch. In the words of a prominent veteran at St Andrew's, 'Bruen has put British golf back on the map'. Without question the excellence of his golf since the first day on which he set foot in St

Andrew's to play in the trials put a morale into the British team which contributed in a very large measure to its eventual success.

The article goes on to describe Cecil Ewing's part in this match, which the reporter describes as a 'fine performance'. He concludes: 'Bruen and Ewing both show that they can keep on producing brilliant golf even when fighting for their lives every inch of the way.'

Some years later, Henry Cotton, in the *News of the World* of 13 April 1941, wrote about Jimmy Bruen's contribution to the 1938 Walker Cup as follows:

When the Walker Cup match was played at St Andrew's in 1938 James Bruen Jr had only just turned eighteen but was the first choice by unanimous opinion. However, as we did not have seven other Bruens it was felt that as usual the strong young American side would slaughter the rest of the weekend golfing amateurs. I was not anxious to play with any one of the team that week because if they did badly after having played with me I knew I would be blamed for having put them off their game. Jimmy, however, was very keen and finally asked the captain, John Beck, if he could play with me. John then came to me and said that he was rather afraid that it might affect Jimmy's play and he did not want to risk it. I felt the same way too but the boy was so keen that John consented so Jimmy and I had our first game. Charlie Stowe and Cecil Ewing, the two members of the team, were the other players in a four-ball game. Jimmy was delighted and far from being put off by playing with the Open champion he went round in 69. Luckily I played well too and we were both round in 69, always a fine score on the old course. In the Walker Cup foursomes ... comparisons which our press made between 'Boy Bruen' and the visitors were far from flattering. There was a period in the middle of 1939 when Jimmy could be with the world's best players. He hit the ball a very long way with all his clubs. He could play all the shots and if he did have a weakness it was his uncertainty on the greens when faced with putts of 4 and 5 feet. His opponent's putting was very sound. I used the past tense there. For I have not seen Jimmy play for two years but had he been able to continue with his big golf this boy would have been one of the greatest players we have had on this side of the Atlantic.

His swing had an unusual sort of kink in it which the critics picked on as being unsound. However, on close analysis I found this kink was a result of an unusually sound grip of the club at the top of the swing. A kink thousands of golfers would pay to acquire.

I had from Jimmy a few months ago a letter in which he told me that to please everybody he had 'ironed the kink' out of his swing and was playing better than ever. This was another answer to his critics by this great golfer, who is so good that he can play any way that you would like. I hope the young genius keeps up his enthusiasm for the game for then we will see some golf.

A golf review in the *Irish Independent* of 11 February 1941, with the heading 'Bruen's Walker Cup', recalled:

When back in 1938 Britain won the Walker Cup, the feat was regarded as in the nature of a modern miracle. And not without some justification.

Two years earlier a team from these islands had gone across to America and on the beautiful Pine Valley course outside Philadelphia was given a devastating trouncing not registering a single win either in the foursome or in the singles. Henry Longhurst, the well-known English golf writer, who had covered the event for his paper, recorded that 'the British side of the scoreboard looked like a daisy chain with 12 noughts one below the other'.

'I settled down,' he recalls, 'to cable the mournful tale and felt more than ever convinced that I should never live to see the Walker Cup in Great Britain'.

Two years later, an American team was at St Andrew's. It was in the main composed of the conquering heroes of Pine Valley. Johnny Goodman was there, and in America they were hailing him as the greatest amateur golfer of the year. Once more, Longhurst was present to record the game, and he was extremely pessimistic. 'On paper they were the most formidable team of amateur golfers that ever gathered on a tee. Being the only writer [at St Andrew's] who had seen this team in action I thought we should be lucky if we got 3 points out of 12 against them and I'm afraid I spread considerable gloom and despondency by saying so'.

But the home team won and Longhurst maintained that the victory was an instance of the psychological element turning the scale of the physical.

'The psychological factor in the person of a nineteen-year-old (in fact eighteen years old) Irishman, James Bruen, began to operate just before the trial matches. From time to time professionals in the Championship had gone round St Andrew's in less than 70 but such scores were still regarded piously as freaks by the Royal and Ancient members. For an amateur, always excepting the great Bobby Jones, such a thing was unheard of.

'Young Bruen began doing it, not once but every day. Some-

times it was 68, sometimes 69. Once it was 66. Eight successive
rounds he played and the worst four of which when added together would have won any Open Championship yet played at St Andrew's. The psychological effect was to demonstrate – that the old
course was not so difficult after all. This boy – he was little more –
set an entirely new standard of golfing ability. Suddenly it dawned
on other players that you don't have to talk with an American
accent to play golf'.

Then Henry Cotton played his part. The famous golfer had
come to report the match for a Sunday paper. He was 'roped in' as
a sort of trainer. He played with members of the British team (I suppose I must call it British although there were two Irishmen, Bruen
and Cecil Ewing, on it) and getting as usual most of the limelight –
the result was that the Americans practised minus the galleries.
That rattled them too, and when Cotton declared that Bruen could
'knock the pants off' Johnny Goodman their morale was shaken.

Bruen did not play Goodman but Hector Thompson did and
licked him by 6 and 4. The Cork boy did not play as well in the
match as he had done in practice but it was Bruen's Walker Cup for
all that.

I read with interest an article in *Golf Monthly* dated May 1963 on
why the British Walker Cup team won the 1938 match:

These are the facts that will clear the mists of memory for those
who were there and for many more who rejoiced in the news sec-
ondhand and painted the scene for the post-war generation. That
is the day that will belong forever to the ten heroes of a triumphant
team … It was the oasis of success which stands out in the desert of
failure before and since. To one like myself a post-war aficionado of
the golfing arena and thus brought up on a diet of bitter defeat,
defeat and again defeat by the American amateur golf machines,
inevitable questions in regard to St Andrew's 1938 are 'Why and
how did we win then?' 'What was so different?' 'We did it then,
why not since?'

… Perhaps it was because of the influence of the flood of
detection on the goggle box that I decided to turn armchair golf
detective and follow the classic method of reconstructing 'the crime'.
What a fascinating path that task led me. I spoke to Captain John
Beck and tracked down half his team. I put it to them – 'Why did
we win? What do you consider were the deciding moments,
matches and shots. Is there anything you would like to tell your
successors in 1963 by way of encouragement?' Let me present the
evidence that we can draw from our conclusions. I did not have to

go far for my first witness just across a neighbouring desk in the golfing press gallery, in fact to my colleague, Leonard Crawley, of the *Daily Telegraph*. Leonard in his forthright way said, 'We had the right side, it was picked after exhaustive trials on the old course a month before the match....

'Then there was this boy Bruen. A golfing genius had suddenly come among us and it gave the side a tremendous lift. In the trials and in practice he worked out on the old course and broke 70 almost every time. He lost the singles to Yates (2 and 1), but he and Harry Bentley gained an enormously important half match in the foursomes ...'

Bruen indeed was a recurring theme in the reflections of his team mates ... The famous loop was in his swing. He hit the ball vast distances and putted like an angel, but he started shakily in the first Walker Cup ordeal ... Bernard Darwin reported in *The Times*, 'Bentley played well and was the glue that stuck the partnership together until his partner had found himself'. If there was one vital stroke in the thirty-six holes then it was Bentley who played it. Cecil Ewing recalled it, so did Gordon Peters and John Beck. It came at the famous road hole at the seventeenth on the old course and the thirty-fifth of the match. Bentley, the indomitable Lancastrian, making his third Walker Cup appearance holed a putt right across the green to square the match, a tram rider, a cricket pitcher, a putt of 20 yards.

What a tumult must have greeted him. Bruen is recorded to have rushed across the green and hugged his partner. The article continues:

Gordon Peters was outwardly so different. Soft-voiced, deliberate-speaking Scot, modest as only those of real achievement can be.

With discerning candour Peters began to answer my 'why we won' question by saying, 'I have often wondered about it too'. He could not resist one of his gentle but penetrating observations against the press: 'All the papers were at great lengths to say that the American team was the worst they had ever sent; your *Daily Express* included'. Gordon was simply marshalling thoughts that were too slow to come but all the more solid for that.

Soon he was saying the reason we won was because we had a good team, a gutsy team – they weren't frightened of winning. That's what is wanted, fellows who can win, who are not afraid to win. I asked Gordon about the personalities of the match and the first comment echoed Leonard Crawley's: 'Boy Bruen gave us a bit of a jab in the arm, the things that boy did were quite incredible'.

The article goes on to quote Cecil Ewing:

'Everybody played well in the match. The reason we have lost so often is that members of the British side on the day don't play as well as they can play and another factor was that we did well in the championship which that year was played before the match. The American team did not run over us at Troon....'

The recollections of John Beck simply confirmed all that I had heard before. 'Bruen gave the Americans a bit of an inferiority complex,' he said. 'They had heard of his phenomenal scoring on the old course before they arrived. In practice he would continue to do these scores. The Scots are pretty hardened golf watchers. Only the best will do them. During the practice they deserted the Americans to go and watch Bruen. He kept on going around in 68. He should have won a single but I made a mistake. I knew that Goodman, their champion, was playing badly but I thought he would still play top and put Bruen in against him.

'But they paid us the compliment of placing Yates who had just won the Amateur at number one and he beat Bruen narrowly.'

The article concluded:

The conclusions were plain. Bruen, Beck's leadership, Bentley's historic putt, ten good men and true who are not frightened of Americans all combined to win the day.

Clearly then, it can be seen that the eighteen-year-old Jimmy Bruen's contribution to the Walker Cup was quite unusual. The combination of youthfulness, marvellous skill at the game of golf and superb confidence was such a psychological tonic to the British team that it cannot be underestimated.

6

Irish Close & British Open Championships 1938

Home from his triumph in the Walker Cup, Jimmy continued to play fantastic golf. There is an interesting cutting from the *Cork Examiner*, 14 June 1938, of the day's golf in Cork Golf Club: 'Bruen goes around in 62'. This was an ordinary club competition which was against par, and Jimmy finished 7 up on bogey par playing off +2, requiring only thirty shots for the first nine and thirty-two for the second nine. The report goes on to say:

> His gross of 62 is easily the best score ever returned at Cork Golf Club, but as the competition yesterday was not played from the championship tees, Bruen's round does not constitute a record.

It is interesting here to record the list of winners, as Jimmy's father, James J. Bruen played a prominent part, finishing fourth behind his son in the singles and winning the four-ball with my father in the afternoon. The results were as follows: James Bruen Junior 7 up; J. F. Wren 3 up; D. C. Morrogh 2 up; J. J. Bruen 1 up; Four-ball Foursomes: G. Crosbie and J. J. Bruen 6 up; F. W. Wren and T. Duncan 6 up; P. Kiely and K. John 5 up; J. Bruen Jr and E. C. Harrington 4 up.

Some days later, Irish amateurs gathered at the Castle Links, Rathfarnham, Co. Dublin, for the Barton Shield, Senior Cup, and Irish Close Championship. Again Cork figured in the final of the Barton Shield, which they retained, and in the final of the Senior Cup in which they were beaten by Portmarnock. The leadership and brilliant golf of Jimmy Bruen was once more apparent.

The Barton Shield opened the proceedings and this event was won by Cork Golf Club who beat their most dangerous rivals, Portmarnock, by four holes in the semi-finals, and Holywood who won the Ulster section in the final by eight holes.

Jimmy Bruen and A. J. Dinan played brilliantly in the morning against W. G. Gill and R. Green, and from the round they had an approximate score of 66, which was eight strokes under the par for the course – regarded by many as the best inland test in Dublin. Apparently the course was playing fairly easy. Nevertheless 66 on any course represents golf of very high standard, particularly in a foursome.

Bruen's driving was the outstanding feature of his game but he also putted very well. Dinan too was sound on and around the greens where, after a disastrous first hole which cost them a 6, Gill and Green did not make a mistake until the fourteenth at which stage the Cork players were only 1 up. Here Green hit a very wild drive under the railings and from that on they became so unbalanced that they lost three of the last four holes.

The golf was also good in the other foursome and it required an approximate 71 by T. A. Healy and B. J. Scannell to finish 1 up on R. Simcox and S. H. McCarthy. The lead changed several times during the round and it was not until the seventeenth that the Portmarnock pair got their winning advantage. A 5 up win by Bruen and Dinan and a one hole loss by Simcox and McCarthy gave Cork a four holes win and a pass into the final. Here we come across one of the few occasions when Jimmy Bruen played indifferently, although they were still to win.

After the morning round against Portmarnock, great things, of course, were expected of Bruen and Dinan in the final. However, Bruen, most uncharacteristically, frequently misjudged chip shots, while Dinan was very uncertain off the tees. At the eighth when the match was all square Dinan hit a drive off the tee close to the seventh green, and it was only a wonderful recovery shot by Bruen within a few yards of the hole that turned what looked like a loss into a win. They also won the ninth and added three more holes on the way home. The winners had an approximate 76 win against 81 for the Holywood players.

Simcox and McCarthy won five of the first six holes in their foursomes but subsequently fell away and it was only two wins near the finish that enabled them to succeed by three holes, giving Cork a win by eight holes, probably a rather flattering win, but nevertheless they retained the title.

The following day, the semi-finals and finals of the Senior Cup were played and Portmarnock again retained their title, beating Cork in the final. In the leading match, Jimmy Bruen played W. G. Gill a +1 handicap player. Giving a brilliant exhibition, the Cork boy won 6 and 5 despite the fact that Gill was level with bogey par for the thirteen holes played. Off the tee Bruen was fully 50 yards outside his opponent while he putted with amazing accuracy on the green that required an amount of knowledge. The par for the first nine holes was 38 but Bruen did them in 32 to be 3 up. Par figures for the first nine: 5, 5, 3, 4, 4, 5, 3, 4, 5 = 38 and Bruen's figures were 4, 3, 3, 4, 4, 4, 3, 3, 4 = 32. When the match finished, Bruen was seven under 4s. Clearly, Jimmy was in tremendous form and was a hot favourite to retain the Irish Close Championship starting the next day.

For the first two matches of the Championship, Bruen, who was the holder, won both his matches with consummate ease. In the afternoon he was out in 33 despite three putts at the eighth and then he was 6 up on Ulsterman A. T. Harty. The match ended on the twelfth with Bruen winning 7 and 6.

According to newspapers at the time, Bruen's next match does not need much description either, the champion was not on his best form. He was out in 38 but was not pressed by T. J. Lawlor whose short game was weak and he was 4 up at that stage. He had 4, 4, 4, 2 for the next four holes and won two of them for a 6 and 5 victory, altogether winning his matches in twenty-five holes.

However, in that day's golf there are one or two other items of great significance. For example, in the second round, Bruen's great opponent, John Burke, was beaten by J. S. Graham, a Belfast player of the Belvoir Park Club, and so Jimmy's main rival went out of the Championship early on. Furthermore, to quote from the *Cork Examiner* of 21 June:

> Another big surprise is the elimination of J. R. Mahon who reached the semi-final of the Irish Open Championship last year. It was not really such a surprise, however, for those who knew of the capabilities of his young conqueror, J. B. Carr, who will be strongly favoured for the Boys' Championship this year and who boasts a 2 handicap at Sutton although only seventeen ...
>
> As is often the case with young players, Carr suffered reaction in the afternoon, and could not get started against J. Morgan who beat him with the greatest of ease by 5 and 3 ...

This form shown by the young J. B. Carr on that day was hardly typical of the great player that he was to become in the not too distant future.

Bruen swept all his opponents aside, and only in the quarter-finals did he have any sort of a difficult match – against G. H. Owens of Skerries, who took him to the eighteenth green.

Bruen had no trouble in disposing of his opponent in the semi-final, by 5 and 4 and so found himself in the final against his old friend and clubmate Redmond Simcox. The *Irish Independent* of 24 June reports:

> The victory of the holder over his fellow Corkman whom he had defeated by 7 and 6 in the final of the scratch cup at Easter was regarded as more or less a foregone conclusion; but Simcox made him fight all the way for his success. At one stage in the second half of the match the issue seemed to be very much in the balance. Simcox failed to seize one or two chances, however, and gradually Bruen got on top again, but up to the last few holes the champion was fighting and fighting very hard.
>
> Simcox's long game was splendid – he was nearly always within a few yards of his long-hitting opponent from the tees and he played some grand iron shots and some cleverly judged chips – but on the greens he was never as sure as Bruen, and it was mistakes here that turned the scales against him.

Jimmy Bruen won his country's Close Championship for the second year in a row. It is not often that two members of the same club and very good friends will play each other in the final of a national championship, I remember years later discussing this point with them. They both agreed. Jimmy, then virtually at the height of his career, wanted of course to retain his championship and in fact would not like to have been beaten by anybody, but nevertheless, as he said to me: 'I would have preferred to play anyone but Redmond'. Redmond, who was a great admirer of Jimmy's told me that he enjoyed that final because at no stage did he think that the unlikely 'fluke' was going to happen and that he was going to beat the great Jimmy. He said he tried as hard as he possibly could but he was pretty sure that even his very best would not be good enough to beat the champion. Both felt that that the result was satisfactory and remembered the day with great affection and pleasure.

So, in early July, Jimmy went to Sandwich to play in the 1938 Open Championship at Royal St George's. The greens were being well watered and looked in splendid condition, but the fairways apparently needed some steady rain. They were hard and brown and in a wind players were finding it difficult to stay on the course. Apart from all the well-known professionals of the day, there were sixty amateurs in the entry and according to the *Cork Examiner* of 4 July:

> The outstanding competitor [amongst the amateurs] is James Bruen, the eighteen-year-old Irish champion. He is credited with a score of 64 in practice. If an amateur is to win, Bruen is the man. James Bruen qualified pretty easily with a 73 and 76 finishing seven strokes behind Johnny Fallon of Huddersfield who had 69 and 73.

The eighteen-year-old Irish champion and Walker Cup player, like most of the competitors in the qualifying rounds, found the task on the homeward half a difficult one. Rain and wind made playing conditions unpleasant. Bruen did the first eight holes in four under 4s despite a 4 at the short sixth. Here he was bunkered. The ninth hole was puzzling, for a new teeing ground had been brought into use. Bruen was going well for eleven holes but he missed a short putt at the twelfth, out of bounds on the thirteenth, which cost him 6, and completed the round in a score of 73. Only thirteen players beat this score on the St George's Links. In the first round the young Irishman had a great 70 to lead the field along with W. J. Cox of Wimbledon Park, Falemagne of France, Johnny Fallon of Huddersfield, E. R. Whitcombe of Bournemouth and Jimmy Adams of Royal Liverpool.

F. J. C. Pignon of the *Daily Mail* takes up the story:

> James Bruen ... made golfing history here today. He lead world-famous golfers in the first round of the Open Championship with a score of 70 and emulated the feat of the world-renowned American Bobby Jones, the only other amateur golfer to lead the Open Championship field in more than a decade. He had a score of 70, six strokes better than the scratch score which is the 'possible golf' for amateur golfers and three strokes better than 'strict par', the score which is supposed to represent perfection. When he walked from the eighteenth green through the applauding gallery all he said was, 'That will do', for he is a dour, reticent young man who always expects to do well, and donning his school blazer, went out to watch Henry Cotton, the holder.
>
> Bruen's achievement was the highlight of a thrilling struggle for a valuable first round lead, which nobody could gain, for accompanying Bruen at the top of the list are five other competitors.

The anticipated fight has commenced and at the end of the day of inspiring golf the issue was almost as open as it was before the first stroke was played. There are no fewer than twenty players who beat the par score of 73. Alfred Perry's name is there with a 71 and so also are two of the Whitcombes, Charles and Reginald, with similar scores. But the champion is not amongst them. Henry Cotton is tied for twenty-eighth place with some other players, among them being Alfred Padgham, another of the favourites. Cotton took the largest gallery of the day when he started out late in the afternoon to break 70 which had been returned by six of his rivals. When I asked him if he felt like breaking the record while he sheltered from one of the several storms just before he started, Cotton said: 'If I can beat the others I shall be satisfied'. But Cotton's hardworking round, as he rightly termed it, occasioned more disappointment than excitement. Bruen's golf was as different from Cotton's as can be imagined. He attacked the hole with every shot within his reach. His youthful courage was sometimes a handicap rather than an asset for he was occasionally too strong. But his great short approaches and his very sound putting counteracted that ...

One of those delicate little pitches which the sturdy young man plays with the delicacy of a woman enabled him to obtain a birdie 3 at the eleventh hole. Over the green at the next he holed a 3-yarder for his 4 getting down with a chip and a putt. At the next a difficult chip from the back of the fifteenth gave Bruen another birdie 4 and having been over the green with a drive and an iron at the seventeenth – a hole some players fail to reach with two wooden clubs – he chipped close enough for another birdie 4.

The eighteenth was even longer than this but Bruen was at the back of the green in 2 and missed the hole by a fraction of an inch for a 3 and a clear lead over the field.

His card read 4, 4, 4, 5, 4, 3, 4, 3, 4 = 35. 4, 3, 4, 4, 5, 4, 3, 4, 4 = 35.

On the same day the golfing correspondent in the *Irish Independent* wrote:

> Bruen has a splendid chance of emulating R. T. Jones, H. Hilton and the late John Ball, the only three amateurs to win the battle. Bruen played sound golf yesterday, his iron shots being particularly accurate ... Having received so many congratulations, no doubt he treasured most the praise of his mother.

It was not to be. Jimmy did not win the Championship. In fact he did not even qualify for the last thirty-six holes, taking what was for him a disastrous 80 in the second round. The following day, the golfing correspondent in the *Cork Examiner* wrote:

> Biggest surprise of the Open Golf Championship was that James
> Bruen, Irish Amateur champion, after leading the field in the first
> round failed to qualify. He had a round of 80, which gave him a
> total of 150, and scores of 148 and under only qualified.
>
> Only one of the three Irishmen competing qualified and that
> was P. J. Mahon of Royal Dublin who had a round of 74 and a total
> of 147. He has only an outside chance of winning the title now …
> Bruen's 80 following a 70 was a tragic experience for so young a
> player. He was probably upset by a 5 at the short eighth where his
> ball was buried in a bunker. He took 40 to the turn and finished
> with two 5s where a couple of 4s would have meant survival.

And so, Jimmy Bruen's first effort to win the Open ended rather
disastrously. But, of course, he had made a big impression and it
was not unexpected that a player of such years would have the
odd bad round. Unfortunately, it came at the wrong time.

I liked a paragraph written by Edward Deane in the *Irish Tatler
and Sketch* in August of that year which read:

> Jimmy Bruen blows up! This crude pronouncement appeared in
> the posters of an Irish daily newspaper, following James Bruen's
> round of 80 at Sandwich which eliminated him from the Open
> Championship. It seems unnecessary to resort to American 'jour-
> nalese' to placard Bruen's failure. Yet in the very crudity of the pro-
> nouncement there lies a subtle compliment. Is it not flattering to a
> golfer of eighteen years to advertise his failure in the Open? Does
> it not imply that everybody expected him to win and his failure
> consequently became 'hot news'?

7

AN IRISH DOUBLE

In July of 1938, Jimmy Bruen went to Portmarnock to play in the Irish Open Championship. This was won by Bobby Locke of South Africa with a total of 292 for four rounds, beating the favourite for the Championship, Henry Cotton, by one stroke in the most thrilling finish fought for the honour since the foundation of the championship on the links in 1927. Locke won as a result of a very unusual collapse of Cotton who had four strokes in hand with four holes to go.

The amateur prize was won by Jimmy Bruen with rounds of 76, 76, 79, 73 for a total of 304. A final round of 73 gave Jimmy Bruen the honour for the second year in succession of being the best amateur, and the only Irish player to finish in front of him was Willie Nolan, the well-known Dublin professional.

In August 1938, the first Inter-Provincial Competition was inaugurated, and it too was played at Portmarnock, on that occasion over thirty-six holes stroke play. The competition was for teams of ten, the best seven scores to count, and was played off the championship tees. Conditions were not ideal for there was a stiff south-east breeze – always the most difficult one to cope with at Portmarnock. At the same time, the standard of scoring was definitely disappointing, given that the players were a picked forty, representing the best amateur talent available in the country.

Moreover, there was point lent to this criticism by the splendid performance of our eighteen-year-old native champion James Bruen whose 70/73, equalling 143, was nine strokes better than the next best aggregate.

Bruen had set the record for the Portmarnock course with his 73 in the Irish Open Championship, and he bettered this by three strokes in the first round.

His golf was by no means immaculate from the tee, but his recoveries from the rough were superb and he never seemed to go astray with those putts of a yard to 3 yards which are so missable. He made only one mistake in this round and that was at the short fifteenth where he failed to hold the green with his tee shot, and was short in an attempt to run up the slope and he took 4. This, of course, was the old eighteenth hole which was in those days a par 5. Bruen's figures for this round were 4, 4, 4, 5, 4, 4, 3, 4, 4, equalling 36 for the first nine, and 4, 3, 3, 5, 4, 4, 4, 4, 3 equalling 34 for a total of 70.

In the afternoon, Bruen started splendidly against the wind with 4, 4, 3 but for once he three putted at the fourth. He might well have had a 5 at the eighth too for he was wide of the green with his second but he laid a superb chip beside the pin, and then rattled down a 4-yard putt at the ninth for a birdie 3. Coming home Bruen was bunkered at the tenth where he took 5, and again at the short twelfth where a 4 went down on his card, but he finished well with two 4s for his second round of 73. This represented wonderfully good golf around this very difficult course. These two rounds of Bruen's gave Munster a great start.

Next best to Bruen both in aggregate and individual score was J. C. Browne who had a bad morning of 80 which included a 7 at the second hole, but returned a fine 72 in the afternoon. Yet another Munsterman was third, again on aggregate and individual scores – this being John Burke with rounds of 74 and 79.

G. H. Owens was the best of the Leinstermen with his 77 and 78, finishing badly each time, and the best score in the Ulster team was Johnny Fitzsimons who had two 78s.

J. R. Mahon played steady golf and came out at the top of the Connaught list also with two 78s. It is interesting to note that J. D. MacCormack, was playing for Connaught, apparently achieved an unusual feat of holing out an iron shot for a 2 at the 430-yard eleventh hole. This feat reminds me that many years later when I had the honour to play J. B. Carr in these same Inter-Pros, when they were match play, Joe Carr did something very similar, only worse. He holed his second shot at the first hole for a 2, and when he came to the eleventh he holed a No. 7 iron for another 2 at that same hole at which J. D. MacCormack also holed out in 2.

It is interesting to record the full results of this competition as there are some very well-known names figuring both at the top and bottom of the list.

Munster: James Bruen Jr, 70, 73 – 143; J. C. Browne, 80, 72 – 152; J. Burke, 74, 79 – 153; W. M. O'Sullivan, 80, 77 – 157; R.

Simcox, 84, 79 – 163; J. Beasley, 77, 87 – 164; F. J. Hannon, 84, 82 – 166; giving Munster a total aggregate of 1098. Other scores: A. J. Dinan, 84, 83 – 169; D. Torrance, 83, 85 – 168; S. H. McCarthy 84 (retired).

Leinster: G. H. Owens, 77, 78 – 155; W. J. Gill, 79, 80 – 159; W. Ffrench, 77, 82 – 159; T. A. Healy, 82, 78 – 160; M. F. Coghlan, 81, 81 – 162; B. J. Scannell 80, 85 – 165; F. A. Lyons, 84, 83 – 167; aggregate 1127. Other scores: J. B. Carr, 82, 86 – 168; C. A. Carroll, 86, 83 – 169; C. J. McMullan, 81, 89 – 170.

Connaught: J. R. Mahon, 78, 78 – 156; J. D. MacCormack, 80, 77 – 157; A. W. Briscoe, 77, 82 – 159; R. C. Ewing, 81, 82 – 163; L. Howley, 81, 83 – 164; D. P. Morris, 84, 81 – 165; T. Lenehan, 84, 89 – 173; aggregate 1137. Other scores: J. O'Driscoll, 87, 86 – 173; P. O'Flynn, 87, 87 – 174; P. O'Byrne, 94, 89 – 183.

Ulster: J. Fitzsimons, 78, 78 – 156; R. W. Barnett, 80, 82 – 162; R. M. Hadden, 85, 79 – 164; S. K. Neill, 84, 82 – 166; J. M. Neill, 86, 82 – 168; H. P. Ritchie, 83, 85 – 168; F. P. McConnell, 87, 82 – 169; aggregate 1153. Other scores: J. McAuley, 79, 91 – 170; R. J. Frizzell 86, 85 – 171; J. McKenna, 89, 85 – 174.

In September of that year, Bruen went to Newcastle, Co. Down to play in the Irish Open Amateur Championship. As a prelude to this championship, there was an 18-hole stroke competition played which was confined to the competitors in the championship which was match play. Jimmy went around this very difficult course in 70 shots and off a +4 handicap, giving him a net score of 74 which won the medal, his nearest rival being G. J. Moore of Beau Desert, off a handicap of scratch with a 75.

Admittedly, Bruen had the best of the weather as a late starter, and the first nine of 37 did not give any promise of the fireworks that were to come. In trouble over the short tenth he hacked the ball out decisively, and rammed his putt for a 3 to start an amazing sequence which saw him home in 33, despite a 5 at the long eighteenth. Here is a list of the leading returns in this competition: J. Bruen, Cork, 70 (+4) = 74; H. F. S. Silcox, Royal Co. Down, 77 (-2) = 75; G. J. Moore, Beau Desert, 75 (Scratch) = 75; J. A. Johnson, SPA. 79 (-3) = 76; J. MacNeill, Royal Co. Down, 79 (-3) = 76; J. P. Cummins, New Lands, 80 (-4) = 76; T. N. Teesdale, West Kilbride, 76 (Scratch) = 76; K. G. Patrick, 76, (Scratch) = 76.; N. A. Kirkpatrick, Manx, 78 (-1) = 77; C. D. Greenhaigh, Turton, 77 (Scratch) = 77; F. A. McMullan, Royal Co. Dublin, 81 (-4) = 77; T.

B. Agnew, Royal Portrush, 79 (-2) = 77.

The following day, the championship proper began and Jimmy made short work of winning all his matches into the last eight. I quote from the *Cork Examiner* for a description of the quarter and semi-final matches:

> James Bruen the eighteen-year-old Cork boy will endeavour today to emulate the feat of L. O. Munn who in 1911 won both the Irish native and Irish Amateur Open championships. He was the only man ever to have done so. Bruen won the native [Irish] title in Dublin in June, and in Newcastle today he contests the final of the Open with J. R. Mahon. Bruen, who is ranked as the best amateur in the British Isles, is in range of yet another distinction. Only once before have the native and open championships of Ireland been won by one golfer in the same year. The Cork boy if he scores the expected victory will also be the first player to win the preliminary stroke competition and the match play. Bruen's opponent is twenty-three years old, and captained the Dublin University team last year. He has a full smooth swing but also a reputation for poor putting ... Bruen's putting, on the other hand, has increased in accuracy during the week, and the Irish champion came onto his game at the right time in the semi-final with K. G. Patrick.
>
> Bruen will start a hot favourite, for throughout the championship he has not been brought further than the fifteenth green and yesterday his victories were by 6 and 5 and 5 and 3 over K. J. Graham and K. G. Patrick respectively.

And so, in the final, Jimmy faced Dr James Mahon, who many years later, would win an Irish Close Championship. The best description I can find of this final was a broadcast on a Northern Ireland programme by a Mr Nash, who was secretary of Portrush Golf Club at the time: ·

> James Bruen of Cork is the new Irish Open Amateur champion. He beat J. R. Mahon of Co. Sligo on the Royal County Down links, Newcastle today by 9 up and eight to play, having been 7 up at lunch interval – and the winner? – ... his name is becoming famous the golfing world over in Britain, the empire, America ... he has gradually become one of the biggest forces in the game and already there are many knowledgeable people who are beginning to rank him in the same category as Bobby Jones and Lawson Little. To be picked to lead Great Britain in the victorious Walker Cup team at an age when most of us are trying to get our handicap down from

the 20s takes a bit of doing. But that is Bruen, quite unassuming, a long hitter and brilliant putter and with a magnificent finish to all his shots. While we are on the subject of Bruen, lets take a look at his opponent J. R. Mahon of Sligo – comparatively unknown to us in Ulster, he is, however, a very fine golfer, a young man too at twenty-four, just finishing his medical studies at Trinity College, Dublin.

... Just before the game began this morning, I was looking at my programme and studying their records in this championship, Bruen had six rounds to play and Mahon had five. Bruen more or less ate up everyone he came in contact with ... the first round he won by 4 and 3, the second 5 and 3, the third 4 and 3, the fourth 5 and 3, the fifth 6 and 5 and the seventh 5 and 4. Talk about scalps.

Then Mahon, well, he beat Banks of Ardeen by 2 and 1, Silcox, Royal County Down 4 and 3, Hannon of Lahinch 2 and 1, McCallum of South Staffs 1 up and yesterday afternoon H. P. Ritchie of Dunmurry, who at Easter this year won the Ulster Scratch singles, by 3 and 2.

So they started at 10 o'clock this morning on the 36-hole battle. The day was perfect. The winds, slight, Newcastle incredibly lovely ... And all of us spectators keyed up to enjoy a battle ... But although Mahon fought, and fought gamely he was no match for Bruen. Bruen was simply terrific. The first hole was halved in 5, the second in 4, the third in 5, decent par figures. Mahon under-clubbing himself once. Bruen in a bunker once. I couldn't help comparing them during those first three holes. Bruen, heavily built, clad in a blue trousers and white shirt and black and white shoes, was watching Mahon intently between shots from the comfort of his shooting stick. Mahon, with a lighter figure and quick attractive smile, concentrating on each shot intent on putting up his best....

... By ordinary standards Mahon is a first-class golfer, but by Bruen's standard he was out of the hunt. Bruen out-drove him, out-ironed him and generally out-putted him.

... At the ninth Mahon messed his second, put it up near the spectators overlooking the green, hooked it out into the bunker on the left of the green and finally, good-naturedly, went up and knocked Bruen's ball into the hole to give the latter a 35 for the first nine holes and be 4 up. And that 35 of Bruen's was terrific stuff, two 5s and all the rest 3s and 4s, and in the final round too. After a week of very strenuous golf, finals don't always show such good stuff.

So to the second nine of the first morning round. At the tenth, Bruen was on from the tee, rather luckily, for his ball rolled back from the rough. Mahon was in the rough near him but his ball did not come back and that was 5 up to Bruen. Then Bruen made a mistake, he put his second at the eleventh into a bunker at the green and got out badly. Mahon made sure of his 4 to reduce Bruen's lead by 1 to 4 up.

At the twelfth there was a dramatic moment or two when both were on in 3 but miles from the hole. Bruen putted first and holed a terrific putt amidst applause. I got out my notebook and sort of licked the end of my pencil preparatory to putting down Bruen 5 up. I waited for Mahon to putt. He putted. His ball looked as though it would never get there, stopped on top of the hole or seemed to and then dropped in, terrific applause but Bruen still 4 up.

At the thirteenth, Bruen, master of every shot, played the most beautiful blind second to within 6 yards of the pin at this difficult hole. Mahon in trouble never looked like halving, and so 5 up.

Then Bruen began hammering the nails in ... we all wondered if Bruen would make a mess of these last three holes as he had never played them in any of his previous matches. But not a bit of it, he finished in par figures losing the seventeenth and winning the eighteenth to be 7 up at the end of the first eighteen and he was around in approximately 71 to Mahon's approximate 79.

And so we went into lunch and came out again to see the further massacre of Mahon. It started immediately, whether it was because Bruen now had a pair of brown trousers on instead of the morning blue pair, I don't know, but he got a couple of birdies at the nineteenth and twentieth and that was 9 up.

... this rather one sided affair ... James Bruen of Cork won his first Open Amateur Championship of Ireland and was warmly applauded. I don't think I'll be prophesying very much if I tell you it won't be his last.

The home internationals were played that year in Royal Portcaul in Glamorgan in Wales. The Irish team did not fare very well being beaten by England and Scotland but beating Wales. On the first day against England, in the top singles, Jimmy Bruen played Frank Pennink whom he defeated by two holes, thus revenging his defeat suffered in the foursomes earlier in the day when, partnered by John Burke of Lahinch, he was beaten by Pennink and Crawley 3 and 1.

The next day, playing against Scotland, Jimmy with a new partner, Bertie Briscoe, again failed narrowly in the foursomes against A. T. Kyle and J. B. Stephenson. In the singles in the afternoon, Scotland paid him the compliment of playing probably their best player, Hector Thompson, on in place of Scottish champion E. D. Hamilton. But again Bruen was beaten. It appears that

Jimmy Bruen's putting was not up to its usual standard. He missed a number of short putts to be beaten 3 and 1. On the third day, against Wales, Bruen had yet another partner, this time playing with the captain of the team, Redmond Simcox. They halved their foursomes against C. P. Eaves and G. T. Wilkie. In the afternoon Jimmy Bruen played Tony Duncan, the Welsh champion, who suffered his first singles defeat in this series. Bruen, the Irish champion, won by 2 and 1 doing the seventeen holes played in two under 4s, and putting brilliantly. However, England, who had five Walker Cup players on their team, won the triple crown.

At the end of that season Henry Cotton wrote about Jimmy Bruen:

> I am still asked how good is Jimmy Bruen, and many people grin when I tell them frankly that in him we have the best young player in golf today; and he is not very far away from the very first flight of professional golf either. Only time will prove how right I am.

8

AMATEUR CHAMPIONSHIP 1939

1939 was to be another incredible year in the career of 'Wonder Irish Golfer' Jimmy Bruen. I notice from a press cutting in February of that year that Jimmy won a competition in Muskerry Golf Club doing a net of 65 off +4 handicap, which in fact gave him a gross of 61. On a course of par 70, and knowing this course even as it was then, this was absolutely fantastic golf. In March of the same year, Jimmy won another competition at Cork Golf Club with a 64 gross off a handicap of +4, giving him a 68 net, the next best score to him being a 70 net. Surely a great start to the new season.

At Easter, in April of that year, the Cork Scratch Cup came around again, and of course Jimmy was the holder. In this competition there is an 18-hole qualifying round. I quote from the *Cork Examiner* of the time:

> In heading the list of qualifiers of the Cork Scratch Cup at Cork Golf Club, Jimmy Bruen, Irish Amateur champion, created a new amateur record for the course beating the score of Redmond Simcox which has stood for seven years. Off the back tees Bruen was around in sixty-seven strokes and an idea of the consistency of his efforts may be gleaned from the fact that his card was made up of thirteen 4s and five 3s. Simcox's record score was also a 67 but the fact that on that occasion he played off one forward tee at the fourth enabled Bruen's return to be regarded as a new record. The old record, also made during a competition, was dated 16 May 1932 … A blustery wind made conditions rather difficult and the only other competitor to break 80 was Redmond Simcox who had a 75. Bruen went on to win his matches and comfortably get into the final where he played Roger Green of Portmarnock and won by 9 and 8 in the 36-hole final. Green, a former Irish international was not a match for the youthful champion who established the commanding lead of 5 holes in the first nine and who never looked in the least like losing his advantage, although Bruen played magnificent golf and the all-round strength of his game was altogether too much for the challenger …

Early in that year as well, Jimmy Bruen played another great round of golf at Muskerry Golf Club which had been altered since his February round of 61. Playing in a 36-hole President's Prize, in the second round on the 5,634-yard course, he created a new record of 66 which was 6 under the new par for the course of 72. His card was made up as follows: Out: 4, 3, 3, 5, 2, 3, 4, 3, 4 = 31. In: 3, 4, 4, 5, 3, 5, 4, 3, 4 = 35. Total = 66. Later on in the year, at the same club in Muskerry, he reduced his own course record from 66 to 63 playing in the qualifying round of the Woodbrook Cup. In this remarkable round Bruen had one eagle and eight birdies and only one bad hole – the short tenth where he took one over par.

His card read: Out: 4, 3, 4, 5, 4, 3, 3, 3, 3 = 32. In: 4, 3, 3, 4, 3, 4, 4, 3, 3 = 31. Total = 63. I notice that on the same afternoon playing in a four-ball Bruen in partnership with N. T. Murphy did 9 up to win that competition as well. What a day out!

So, in May, Jimmy Bruen went to Hoylake to play in the Amateur Championship, and in the second round met Leonard Crawley, another famous Walker Cup player. F. C. Pignon of the *Daily Mail* wrote:

This was youth's proud day at the Amateur Golf Championship meeting here at the Royal Liverpool Club's sunbathed links. Two nineteen-year-old players, James Bruen of Cork and Tom Hiley of South Port and Kenneth Tom, seventeen-year-old Essex Boy's champion, stole most of the admiration of the big crowd for their amazing feats of golfing skill.

Bruen figured in what may be regarded as a key match to the Championship when he defeated Leonard Crawley, a golfer of vast experience and undoubted ability in a most convincing manner. It was a battle in which Crawley was enmeshed in the stranglehold grip of Bruen's relentless accurate golf, and his putter, the only club that might have saved Crawley, served only temporarily to stave off his inevitable eclipse.

Young Bruen, trained to the moment and having lost about two stone in the process, is a sturdy fellow, but Crawley, hero of many famous golf and cricket matches with his sandy hair, bristling moustache and powerful build, looked every inch a powerful athlete. But physical strength was not to be the deciding factor, although on the whole Bruen had slightly the better of the long driving.

It was the fact that the youth so frequently outplayed his

opponent with perfectly controlled second shots of giant length that gave him his advantage. Of the two it was the more experienced golfer who displayed the nervous tension of the great match, and he did so by frequently leaving the long putt short or failing to hole putts the length of his club. Bruen is a poker-faced youth who displays neither pleasure nor annoyance, so that it was impossible to read in his face any sign of anger when his long drive to the second hole finished in a bunker. He simply stepped into the sand and banged the shot of about 150 yards onto the green.

This shook Crawley who proceeded to take 3 putts. From that point Bruen was always in the lead …

In the next round Bruen beat the Scottish champion, E. D. Hamilton, and established himself as favourite for the title, and Pignon, writing in the *Daily Mail*, observed: 'Before he played a shot in this championship I said I would not be surprised if the Irish youth won the title. Now, having watched his triumphant golf, I shall be surprised if he does not win'.

He out-drove Hamilton sometimes by 60 yards, and length counts on this giant course. He played an occasional loose iron, but always retrieved it by deft pitching and putting.

Bruen was struggling until he came to that loop of long holes at the far corner of the course. He holed a long putt to gain the lead with a birdie 4 at the long eighth, won the tenth with a chip and a putt and became 3 up with a 3 at the eleventh. In the next two rounds, Bruen had two 5 and 4 victories. Again I quote F. C. Pignon:

Bruen's progress continued at the expense of two young players, Ronald Inglis a brilliant nineteen-year-old Scot and John Alan Graham, a young member of the famous Hoylake golfing family. Inglis put up a magnificent fight for a while but he was down all the way in spite of golf that would have beaten many other competitors. Bruen went out in 35 and was 3 up and lost only one hole in the whole match – the short thirteenth. But he was still 4 up and finished the match with a cruel eagle 3 – a drive and a No. 4 iron and a 4-yard putt to win the 500-yards fourteenth. Graham was unable to put up anything like such a fight. He lost three of the first four holes and was 6 down at the eighth and gained his first success of the match when he holed a chip for an eagle 3 at the ninth. But Bruen was dormie 5 and won at the fourteenth. Now into the last eight, Jimmy Bruen met fellow Walker Cup player, Scot, Alex Kyle, a thirty-two-year-old textile designer in Bradford. He defeated the Irish champion by 1 up in one of the most extraordinary matches of the Championship or any championship.

The defeat of Jimmy Bruen was a sore disappointment not only to Irish golfers but many other golfers at Hoylake, for certainly the Championship had lost an outstanding personality. The Cork boy was not at his peak but the breaks of the day were all against him and the luck of the game was with Kyle....

In the history of the Amateur Championship it will be difficult to equal the story of those wonderful successful recoveries of Kyle at so advanced and vital a stage of a tie. Bruen's scoring was the highest round he had played in a match or in practice at Hoylake taking 76 to go around the course.

After this championship another golfing correspondent in an Irish newspaper wrote:

Jimmy Bruen did not win the British Amateur Championship after all, but he did something more remarkable still – in defeat he established himself as the finest amateur golfer since the days of Bobby Jones. Accepting the press as the mouthpiece of British golfers, and all credit must be given to their high sense of sportsmanship, Bruen has been acknowledged for the second year in succession as the season's most outstanding player ... the praise accorded him both before and after his defeat was without parallel and with one voice the critics expressed the keenest disappointment at his unlucky sixth round defeat ... The discussion aroused by the amazing finish to Bruen's match against Kyle will not soon die down and it is the direct cause of suggestions from certain quarters that the Championship conditions should be altered. One that is not likely to meet with much support is that the matches should be played over thirty-six holes for the reason that such a course would entail qualifying rounds in different areas to enable the select few to participate in the Championship proper. What is of great importance is that an outstanding case has arisen of the unfairness of the stymie. Here we have an instance of a player reaching the green with two perfect shots and finishing within easy holing distance only to find himself stymied by an opponent who played his third shot from a bunker guarding the green. It is possible if not probable that this cruel piece of ill-luck deprived Jimmy Bruen of the British Amateur title ...

Jimmy Bruen was to wait a further seven years before he could play in the British Amateur Championship again because the war intervened. On 28 May, in the *News of the World,* Henry Cotton wrote a piece about Jimmy Bruen:

> Now for the last eight of the contestants [in the Amateur Champion-ship]. First a word about the outstanding amateur of today and for several years to come as far as I can see – James Bruen Jr from Cork or 'young Jimmy' to everyone.
>
> Last year I was impressed by his wonderful golf in the Walker Cup series at St Andrew's and also by his fine judgment in picking up shots as they were required. To those who saw him then it may now sound odd when I say this modest boy of nineteen is a much improved golfer from the Bruen of St Andrew's in 1938.
>
> You have all heard of the dangerous kink in the top of his swing, but Bruen, being the studious golfer, has during this winter got rid of it by improving his grip. His swing today is probably the sim-plest in the game and most orthodox. To me he is a joy to watch. He stands up to the ball with a definite pigeon-toed stance, holds the club with the Vardon grip, hands are held high and he uses a left hand glove, has a short but very wide back swing with a slight flail action on the way down.
>
> All this accounts for his accuracy, and his length comes from a terrific speed at impact. In fact I know there is not another player in the game today with the same speed of club-head as this boy. All his shots are hit straight at the stick and high, proving that the open-face method which he uses is the soundest. I know many long hitters but I do not know one as straight or as long as Jimmy Bruen. To my mind he is a golf genius and will be a danger at St Andrew's in the Open for, besides being an improved golfer, he likes the course and he is the only man who plays the old course in a new way, disregarding old traditions and precedents, this almost applies to all his game.

Henry Longhurst writing about the same Amateur Champion-ship says:

> With all due respect to the winner, I have to confess that I shared the general opinion that Bruen stood head and shoulders above them all, British or American … For myself I should rate Bruen in the highest professional class and shall not be in the least surprised if he wins the Open.

The 1939 Irish Close Championship was held at Rosses Point golf course, Co. Sligo. This fine west of Ireland golf course is well known to many golfers both in Ireland and in England, and famous for the West of Ireland Championship played here every Easter and, of course, is the home of Cecil Ewing.

Nobody, it seemed on paper, could stop Jimmy Bruen that year from winning his third Irish Close Championship, but there were many other fine Irish golfers in the field as well as Bruen. Cecil Ewing and John Burke, both Walker Cup players, along with Roy McConnell, J. B. Carr, W. M. O'Sullivan, G. H. Owens, B. J. Scannell, and the previous year's runner-up, Redmond Simcox. The description, in the *Cork Examiner* of Tuesday 30 June, of his first match must be an understatement:

> James Bruen, the holder, has become better acquainted with this testing course and is beginning to like it very much. In his match today in the second round to which he got a bye he played steadily and well. He holed the first nine in 31 – 5 under bogey and knocked out his opponent, G. Titterington of Malone, by 8 and 7.

In the third round Jimmy beat C. W. Robertson of Portmarnock by 5 and 4. He was again in good form when he played W. M. O'Sullivan of Killarney in the fourth round – going out in 35 he turned 2 up. He finished the match impressively with a one under par 4, 3, 4, run to beat O'Sullivan 4 and 3. The Wednesday afternoon was to see the defeat of the three Walker Cup players in the field. J. B. Carr beat Cecil Ewing; B. J. Scannell beat John Burke; and Gerry Owens beat Jimmy Bruen. The big surprise – the achievement of the seemingly impossible – occurred when Gerry Owens accounted for the Corkman at the seventeenth.

The day was one of brilliant sunshine but with a faint breeze from the north, wholly different from the previous day's conditions when Bruen put up brilliant performances against a tearing northwesterly wind which disconcerted most of the other contenders. On the Wednesday the course was easier.

The home figures were – Bruen: 4, 5, 5, 3, 4, 4, 3, 4 = 32. Owens: 3, 5, 4, 3, 4, 3, 3, 3 = 28 for eight holes. That gave Gerry Owens a 3 and 1 win over the great Bruen. In the last eight of this championship was probably the first time that Joe Carr met Cecil Ewing – they were, of course, to meet many times in later years and the *Cork Examiner* describing that match said 'Cecil Ewing could not stand up to the seventeen-year-old Carr's putting which was phenomenal. He had only one putt on eleven greens and sank five 20-footers in succession and he won easily on the sixteenth'.

The young university student, Brennie Scannell, also another up and coming player, beat John Burke decisively by 4 and 3.

Gerry Owens played Roy McConnell in the final and went on to win the championship. However, getting back to the Bruen/Owens match, an examination of the figures shows that Gerry Owens was four under 4s over this very stiff course. Indeed, it took figures like that to beat the Jimmy Bruen of 1939. And so, Gerry Owens had the distinction of being the man to stop Jimmy Bruen from a hat-trick of Irish championships.

9

69, 69 IN THE OPEN

The British Open was played in 1939 at St Andrew's and, before the Championship was played at all, Thomas Woodrooffe, writing in the *Sunday Despatch* on 2 July under a large heading across five columns, said, 'Boy Bruen is third favourite for the Open'. Woodrooffe's article went on to say:

As you read this, two sons of Éire are girding their loins for the fray, Jack Doyle and James Bruen, and both from Co. Cork. Whereas Doyle hits his opponent's chin (or thin air) harder than any, James Bruen of Muskerry clouts a golf ball with more aplomb and accuracy than the average. Five weeks ago he was nineteen, yet he is third favourite for the Open Golf Championship which begins today at St Andrew's; and no amateur has set tongues wagging so hard at many a nineteenth since Bobby Jones first came over here and broke his clubs across his knee in a rage over a bad round. Jones swore he'd make amends for that exhibition, if you remember, and he did. He came back and won our Open at St Andrew's, the Alma Mater of golf. If Bruen wins he will be the first Irishman in history to have done so, perhaps because they lack the plodding diligence of the Scot.

Championship golf today is an applied science; the leisurely days of James Braid and Sandy Heard are over. Heard by the way will be appearing at his native St Andrew's for the last time. He is seventy-two.

Bruen is undoubtedly the greatest amateur golfer in the world today ... but he has yet to win the British Amateur Championship. Bruen's strength lies in stroke play – very different from match play – and the four rounds of stroke play in the open may be his meat.

He is far and away the greatest stroke player amongst all the amateurs – but nineteen is an early age to take on the professionals who specialise in it. Four rounds of intense concentration – you can't let up for a second – one shot carelessly played, a little bit of bad luck in your round and your chances in the Championship are gone for a year.

No wonder so many golfers suffer from dyspepsia or nervous indigestion. Bobby Jones at the end of a round was sick as a cat. James Bruen, however, loves St Andrew's. While he was practising for the Walker Cup last year he returned 282 for four rounds, 68, 71, 71 and 72 – good enough incidentally to have won any Open ever played at St Andrew's – it is three strokes better than Bobby Jones' record in the Open in 1927.

Even though these figures were only done in practice at St Andrew's … they are sufficiently imposing to make us wonder whether another child prodigy isn't among us.

He'll be tested in the fire with Henry Cotton, Bobby Locke, Reg Whitcombe and Lawson Little, who won the Amateur here two years ago ...

[Bruen] is 5ft 11.5" and weighs 11 stone instead of the 13.5 he weighed a year ago – thanks to a system of physical training recommended by Henry Cotton ...

He is quiet and for one of his age has the most amazing control of his emotions which accounts for his greatness at stroke play.

Cyril Tolley has described him as the greatest golfer of our time. If he doesn't win the Open this year he still has plenty of years left. St Andrew's is rather sniffed at nowadays by the experts – the professionals can reach most of the greens in a drive and a chip.

St Andrew's doesn't compare with Hoylake and the other championship courses for length, but though tradition dies hard, far seeing golfing people in the north – where they've forgotten more about golf than we'll ever learn – have realised that some day soon a new and greater St Andrew's will be necessary.

In the Bruen scrapbook there is an old course of St Andrew's card pasted in, dated 30 June 1939, which presumably was a practice round on the old course before the Open Championship. The card is duly signed and the figures read: the first nine – 4, 3, 4, 4, 5, 4, 4, 3, 4 = 35; second nine – 3, 3, 3, 3, 4, 5, 3, 4, 3 = 31; total 66. A handicap of +4 is added giving a net score of 70. And that was some round of golf. There is an x marked opposite the two holes, fifth and fifteenth, the only two 5s on that card, and along the white margin is written in ordinary handwriting three putts on these two greens. And so it appears that if he had not taken those three putts he would have been around the old course on that day in sixty-four shots.

For the next four days the young Irish boy was to hit the headlines in most newspapers, certainly in the British Isles and probably in the world. Also he was to reach what was arguably the highest peak of his already fantastic golfing career. The *Irish Press* of 4 July, for example, had the following heading: 'Jimmy

Jimmy drives off the first tee at St Andrew's in 1938.

The Bruen swing 1938.

M. P. FitzPatrick, Jimmy, Billy McMullen, and Joe Carr.

Jimmy wins the British Boy's Championship at Birkdale.

Jimmy wins his first Irish Close Championship at Ballybunion in 1937.

Jimmy with Harry Bentley, 1938.

The Bruen Loop at the top of the back swing.

The Illustrated

SPORTING

and DRAMATIC News

Boy Golf Prodigy—James Bruen of Ireland

Cover of The Illustrated Sporting and Dramatic News, *1938.*

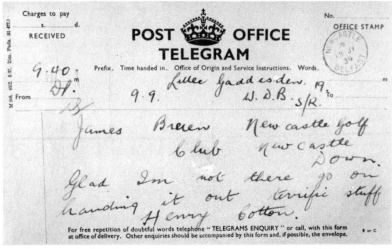

Telegram received by Jimmy from Henry Cotton after record score of 66 in the first round of the Irish Open in 1939.

Irish Team, 1937: Back [l/r]: Gerry Owens, John Neill, Clifford McMullen, Cecil Ewing, Billy O'Sullivan, Bertie Briscoe, John Burke. Front [l/r] John Fitzsimmons, Jimmy, Redmond Simcox [Capt.], James Mahon, Joe Brown.

Jimmy wins his second Irish Close Championship at the Castle Golf Club, Dublin, 1938. Jimmy is with Runner-up Redmond Simcox – in the background are George Crosbie, Sr, President of Golfing Union Of Ireland and Mrs Maureen Crosbie – all four were members of Cork Golf Club, Little Island.

Red Cross Exhibition Match at Cork Golf Club, 1940: [l/r] John McKenna, Redmond Simcox, Jimmy and Jack Higgins.

Presentation to Jimmy – British Amateur Champion, Birkdale 1946.

Bruen, Carr and Ewing – three great Irish golfers.

The Jimmy Bruen putting stance [note left elbow and pigeon-toe stance].

Finish of the Bruen Swing.

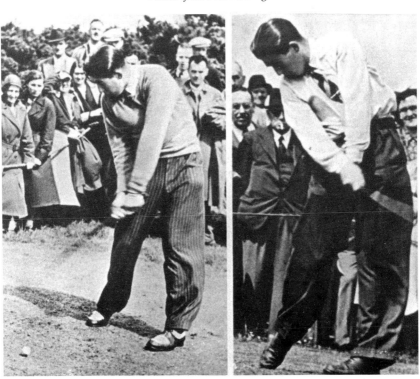

Just before, and just after the impact.

Jimmy with his two mentors and friends:
[l] Jack Higgins [Cork] and Henry Cotton [Royal Mid Surrey].

Henry Cotton drives off the first tee at Cork Golf Club – watched by McKenna, Bruen and O'Sullivan. Among the audience were Mick Power, P. McGrath, Lord Mayor of Cork, Gus Healy, and Connie Griffin – Bruen's famous caddie [wearing dark cap, left centre of audience].

Exhibition Game, Cork Golf Club, 1953. [l/r]: John McKenna, Henry Cotton, Jimmy and Billy O'Sullivan.

Exhibition Game, Cork Golf Club, 1953. [l/r]: Henry Cotton, Jimmy, G. F. Crosbie and T. W. Egan

The great Fred Daly [Open Champion 1947] with Jimmy examining shoes in Saxone Shoe Company.

Two of Ireland's greatest amateurs
Joe Carr and Jimmy Bruen at Cork Golf Club.

Mrs Nell Bruen.

*Below: George Crosbie
with Jimmy, Cork Scratch Cup 1953.*

Jimmy in action.

Bruen, 69, burns up St Andrew's'. The report continues:

> Jimmy Bruen, nineteen-year-old Irish amateur; Lawson Little of
> America and Percy Alliss (Peter's father), British Ryder Cup play-
> er, were the record makers at St Andrew's yesterday and shared the
> lead on the first qualifying round of the British Open Golf Cham-
> pionship. Alliss established a record of 69 on the new course and
> similar records were returned by Little and Bruen on the old course
> which will be used for the competition proper tomorrow ... the
> young Irishman had the distinction of creating an amateur record
> for the course, as Bobby Jones did in 1927, with a 68. The compari-
> son between the two feats, separated by so many years is useless
> but Bruen, who hit the first drive of the championship, made a
> magnificent recovery from a disastrous start and his score can be
> regarded at least the equal of Jones' 68.
>
> Bruen who is considered to have an excellent chance of win-
> ning the title had two 6s in the first five holes but afterwards he
> played such powerful and accurate golf that he was six under 4s for
> the remaining thirteen holes. In one great spurt around the loop he
> had four 3s in succession driving the green at the 360-yard ninth
> and putting a short chip shot dead for another birdie at the 312-
> yards tenth.
>
> Bruen pitched to within 6 feet of the hole for a birdie 4 at the
> fourteenth, holed a putt of similar length for a birdie 4 at the sev-
> enteenth and finished a grand round by laying a niblick shot 4 feet
> from the hole for a 3 at the eighteenth. The Irishman's position as
> leader was unchallenged for four hours. Then Little, a broad-shoul-
> dered player who won the English amateur championship twice in
> succession, equalled Bruen's score by coming home in 32 with 2s at
> the eleventh and twelfth. A 10-yard putt gave him a birdie at the
> world's famous short hole, the eleventh, and then he drove the
> green at the 314-yard twelfth then holed from 4 yards for an eagle
> 2 under par. He finished just as Bruen had done by laying his ap-
> proach shot dead at the home hole for a birdie 3. The two cards
> read as follows:
>
> Bruen – Out: 4, 6, 3, 4, 6, 3, 4, 3, 3 = 36. In: 3, 3, 4, 4, 4, 4, 4, 4, 3
> = 33. Total 69.
>
> Little – Out: 4, 5, 4, 4, 5, 4, 4, 3, 4 = 37. In: 4, 2, 2, 4, 5, 4, 4, 4, 3 =
> 32 also totalling 69.

Bruen left the course to the cheering of the spectators with the
comment 'That will do for a start'. On the next day on the New
course Jimmy did another 69 and set another course record. The
headlines read: 'James Bruen the hero of St Andrew's, joint holder

of record on both courses now shares honours with Bobby Jones';
'Bruen beats world's best professionals, leads Henry Cotton and
Lawson Little by four strokes'; 'Magic putting for another 69
puts him on a par with Bobby Jones'. How well this round of golf
is described in *The Scotsman* on Wednesday, 5 July:

> With the wizardry that held 3,000 spectators spellbound, James
> Bruen the amazing nineteen-year-old Irish phenomenon complet-
> ed the new course here this evening in sixty-nine strokes and now
> heads the qualifying list of 129 competitors in the open golf cham-
> pionship, including the crack professionals of this and other coun-
> tries, with a remarkable aggregate of 138.
>
> Not only did he break the old course record yesterday with a
> 69 but he had a New Course record set up in the first round by
> Percy Alliss completely at his mercy tonight when he hit a prodi-
> gious drive of about 300 yards to the eighteenth hole, leaving him-
> self only a simple pitch. Anywhere on the green would have prob-
> ably secured him the extraordinary duality in records for these
> famous links, but he hooked the pitch, chipped about 2 yards be-
> yond the flag and then missed the putt ... his golf has placed him
> as many as four strokes in front of Henry Cotton, number one
> favourite, for the Championship and Lawson Little, strongest of the
> challengers from the United States. Percy Alliss and Johnny Bulla
> from Chicago came up to fourth place with 143, Reg Whitcombe the
> title holder is one stroke behind that total and Jack MacLane, ex-
> Scottish Amateur champion and Martin Pose, the spearhead of the
> Argentinean team two strokes behind with 145 ... Can Bruen keep
> it going? ... he is something rare in the game ... There is more bril-
> liance where that of these two days' ties came from, and the only
> qualification attached to it is the doubt whether he can stick it when
> the pressure comes on. It is a supremely big task for one who is lit-
> tle more than a boy. At Hoylake before his other championship he
> was breaking 70 in round after round and in the Walker Cup trial
> play and practice last year he did eight rounds any four of which
> would have won any championship yet played on the old course
> ... His mental attitude to the whole thing is in itself priceless and is
> something neither the oldest inhabitant of this golfing centre nor
> the club's oldest member has ever seen excelled. If he can keep his
> form for the next three days it is difficult to imagine him beaten....
> ... It was after 7 p.m. when he holed out although the draw re-
> versed from yesterday's order sent him out last on the new course.
> Play was so unduly prolonged what with the deliberate methods
> of his partner and the delay due to the big crowd which had to
> move and settle, move and settle again ... The exhibition given by

this Irish wonder youth was one thrill after another, glorious long driving, chips and putts of the best possible class, and through it all the coolest person present was Bruen.

The more one sees of him the more the wonder grows ... The weather was in his favour and the wind which had been troubling earlier campaigners fell away towards the evening and there was a dull light under a heavy sky which threatened a deluge which fortunately did not come ...

... who is going to whisper anything that might even savour of criticism or complaint of his wonderful 69. The details of his card of this afternoon are – Out: 4, 3, 4, 3, 3, 4, 4, 4, 4 = 33. In: 4, 3, 5, 3, 3, 4, 5, 4, 5 = 36. Total 69.

Another newspaper of the day wrote of that performance:

Bruen is the first amateur from these islands to accomplish the best score in the preliminary stages since a qualifying test was instituted in 1920 ... triumph has enhanced his prospects of becoming the first amateur from these islands to win the title since 1897. Bruen's brilliant golf was phenomenal for a youth in his teens. He seemed oblivious of the rushing spectators and intent only upon hitting every shot correctly ... he must be regarded as a modern prodigy of the links.

St Andrew's is his favourite course and it was on the old links last year that he played seventy-two holes in 284 strokes ... He has every claim to be regarded as the new 'Bobby Jones'. Few spectators expected him to deliver a strong challenge to the professional stars and it was astounding to see him finish so many strokes ahead.

There is another nice little paragraph in the *Daily Record* 'While some chat to players, Mother Bruen stays indoors to watch':

More shy of publicity than any Garbo of Hollywood is Mrs James Bruen of Cork. Each day at St Andrew's, Mrs Bruen has followed her son around the course, and then goes back to her hotel overlooking the links where she can watch the other players finish, without getting caught up in the crowd. Her son, on the other hand, walks around the course after his game chatting with the other players and occasionally going along to try out some new clubs in the large marquee near the course. Mrs Bruen has her own ideas about publicity and although she takes a keen interest in her son's game she sometimes wishes he had been just a little older before getting into the limelight of championship golf.

My father, along with a number of other members from Cork Golf Club who were present at St Andrew's that day, used to tell a story of an incident that happened that evening after Jimmy had done his two 69s. Apparently some of the leading professionals, because they had been playing themselves and had not had an opportunity of seeing this young phenomenon, Bruen, asked him to go out on the practice ground and hit some shots for them. My father and his friends thought that this was a very bad thing and would tire Jimmy as the championship proper was starting the following day. They apparently approached Mrs Bruen to stop him but she declined to interfere. Apparently Jimmy spent something like a couple of hours that evening hitting golf balls, and my father always held that it cost him the Open Championship.

However, be that as it may, after the qualifying rounds the leader board read as follows: On 138 James Bruen Jnr, Cork, 69, 69. On 142 Henry Cotton, Ashridge, 69, 73; Lawson Little, Bretton Woods, USA, 69, 73. On 143 P. Alliss, Ferndown, 74, 69; J. Bela, Chicago, USA, 71, 72. On 144 Reg Whitcombe, Parkstone, 72, 72. On 145 J. MacLane, Buchanan Castle, 73, 72; M. Pose, Argentina 73, 72. On 146 J. Fallon, Huddersfield, 71, 75; J. Bailliew, Royal Melbourne, Australia, 73, 73. On 147 A. J. Isherwood, Warrington, 76, 71; S. A. Easterbrook, Knowle, 75, 72; A. Compston, Coombe Hill, 74, 73; A. D. Locke, South Africa, 73, 74; A. Lees, Dore Totley, 73, 74; S. S. Scott, Hartlepoole, 74, 73; L. B. Ayton Jnr, Stoneham, 74, 73; J. Burton, Hillside, 73, 74; C. A. Whitcombe, Crews Hill, 73, 74. On 148, J. A. Jacobs, Lindrick, 73, 75; H. Thompson, William Wood, 70, 78; J. J. Busson, Pannell, 75, 73; W. J. Branch, Leicestershire, 75, 73. On 149 J. Knight, Bloxwich, 77, 72; J. H. Busson, Formby, 76, 73; E. Bertolino, Argentina, 74, 75; A. Perry, Leatherhead, 74, 75; D. J. Kyle, Royal & Ancient, 75, 74; W.D. Smithers, Sunningdale 77, 72. On 150 E. Serra, Uruguay, 74, 76; H. B. Rhodes, South Herts, 76, 74; J. C. Wilson, Cowder, 75, 75; B. Gadd, South Shields, 74, 76; G. Telford, West Sussex, 74, 76; L. Holland, Gerrard's Cross, 72, 78; A. G. Matthews, Roehampton, 74, 76; G. Chapman, Princes, 76, 74; A. Sutton, Leigh, 71, 79; W. Shankland, Templenewsam 76, 74; F. Bradbeer, Barnham & Barrow, 78, 72; S. S. Field, Dunstable Downs, 78, 72; A. T. Kyle, Sandmore, 73, 77. On 151 B. Sheppard, Radleth, 77, 74; W. Davis, Dumfries and County, 78, 73; M. Faulkner, unattached, 78, 73; W. J. Cox, Wimbledon Park, 79, 72; A. Castanon, Argentina, 72, 79; M.

Cheurio Argentina 76, 75; L. McPherson, East Renfrew, 78, 73; D. J. Rees, Hindhead, 76, 75; D. Cameron, Kirkintilloch 75, 76; T. Pierpoint, Highgate, 78, 73.

Jimmy Bruen did not win the Championship but that story is best told by the journalists of the day. On 5 July the golfing correspondent in the *Cork Examiner* wrote

> The nineteen-year-old Cork champion started out in record style and everything seemed set for another spectacular display but fate and the crowds ruled otherwise.
>
> Thousands of spectators lined the fairway when Bruen drove off while others had already gone ahead to see him at some other vantage points. After making an almost superhuman start on his first championship round, tired toward the finish with a searching crowd talking all around him, he returned a 72. When at the ninth hole, there was every prospect that he would equal or even lower his own record of 69.
>
> It is impossible for anyone who does not know this 'city' of golf to comprehend the scene. Bruen came down the steps from the Royal & Ancient clubhouse at 3.30 and what met his gaze was a vast concourse packing all the path along the railings and around the first green ... Even before Bruen drove off his first tee shot, spectators, realising the difficulty of seeing him play the first, had gone on to take up vantage points behind the second green.
>
> The crowd had gathered from all parts of Scotland to watch the 'Hibernian Wonder Golfer'. The lad surveyed the scene quietly, almost nonchalantly. He gazed around at the extended amphitheatre of humanity. The crowd who wanted to bring him in the leader was strangely quiet and the pleasant rolling of the breakers on St Andrew's Bay made the only sounds. Bruen made little half swings with his driver and when the starter called 'James Bruen, (Cork) play on', stepped out and without ado he immediately electrified the crowd by crashing his first blow away ... He took a mashie niblick, almost hit the flag, and the ball, when it landed, actually jumped back 2 feet to draw up a few inches from the hole. A 3 opened the tally and he nearly had a 3 at the second where he deliberately played away from the flag to the right side of the green to avoid the traps, but nearly holed a 15-yards putt. It was a 4 and then followed a couple of birdie 3s. Bruen thus had opened 3, 4, 3, 3, and this compared with Bobby Jones' start in 1930 when the American had 3, 4, 3, 2 ... Bruen got a birdie 4 at the long fifth and when everything looked set for more fireworks with easy holes ahead he went off his long game in direction but not in length. At the sixth he was amongst short heather and the first five went down. He was a way

off line driving to the seventh but he gathered the par 4 and kept par at the eighth and ninth to turn in 33. His figures out were 3, 4, 3, 3, 4, 5, 4, 3, 4 = 33.

That was grand going but a 4 at the tenth was poor. He was through the green at the short eleventh and took 4. He had not a good drive at the twelfth and now from this point he did not get the figures expected. The crowd was streaming across the fairway. The stewards were shouting orders and Bruen had to wait on tee after tee, sometimes as long as five minutes. He took three-and-a-half hours to go around and it must have shaken him. At the fourteenth he hit a courageous shot right across 'Hell' but his pitch was off the line and he took a 5, then came two par 4s. Bruen could always count on picking up a 3 at one or the other of these holes.

Then came the worst of all at the road hole. He hit a herculean drive away across the railway shed but pulled his mashie. Most players were using full irons on their second. His shot got a nasty kick on one of the hummocks and nearly went into a bunker. He ran up a 6. In the last hole Bruen hit what was believed the longest drive of the day. He slammed his mashie niblick 3 yards from the hole and the putt just turned off for the 3. Bruen walked off the green with his head a little down. It had been a trying ordeal and the crowd who had gone out to hero worship had in their very enthusiasm taken the edge off his game. Bruen's figures for the second half were: In – 4, 4, 4, 4, 5, 4, 4, 6, 4 = 39, total 72.

Bruen is two strokes behind the leaders. It is not serious with three rounds to go but it all looked so glorious and rosy earlier on and it seemed as if he would easily lead. After the round he was soon his cheery self. Given reasonable elbow room he will give of his best on the morrow.

Most golfers I think would be very pleased indeed to get around the old course at St Andrew's in 72, but it seems that this score on that day was very disappointing for the great Jimmy Bruen. They had got so used to him breaking 70 that 72, still only two strokes behind the leaders of the Open, seemed mediocre to his followers.

On 7 July, again in the *Cork Examiner*, we read:

(For his third round) He was among the early starters and there was evidence of his popularity for the large crowd who waited to see him drive off and grew in number until near the end he had 7,000 in his wake. The first hole was a par and at the second he was nearly down in 3. He drove into the whins at the third and was fortunate in finding his ball lying in grass from which he was able to

execute a deft pitch which finished 3 yards from the pin. He missed
the putt but got his regulation 4. At the fourth and fifth holes his
driving was not good ... He was fortunate at the long fifth where
he pulled away to the left and found his ball clear but on the side
of a bunker. He was able to take wood again but could not reach
the green, another 5 going down. Bruen at this point was two over
4s.

Holing a 4-yards putt he got a birdie 3 at the sixth but his second to the seventh finished in the rough and he took a 5. The eighth
and ninth he matched 'old man par' to turn in 37. Bruen's figures
were: Out – 4, 4, 4, 5, 5, 3, 5, 3, 4, to be out in 37.

He started homeward in a blaze of glory. He drove to the
fringe of the tenth hole pitched up dead and got a birdie 3. He
played the eleventh, the short Eden hole, with great care, finishing
below the green to avoid the bunkers, ran up dead and had a par
3. Two orthodox 4s followed. He played the fourteenth in the teeth
of the wind ... hitting two full shots right across the 'Beardies' and
'Hell'. He did not chip up too accurately but got his 5 all right. At
the fifteenth and sixteenth Bruen was obviously determined to
keep away from the railway which is a dangerous out of bounds
and he did not go for the straight line but played away to the left.
He got 4 at both and was now level 4s with two to go.

From the tee to the seventeenth he hit a wonderful drive right
across the railway sheds, a tremendous distance and his second
shot he played with accuracy to the bottom of the green. It was the
right shot to play in order to keep clear of the bunker and avoid
going over the road. He took his putter for his third shot ... hit the
putt up the green which at the top has a little fold in the ground
which turns towards the bunker in the face of the green. Bruen hit
the ball seemingly perfectly and when it came to this deceptive
curve at the crown of the hollow an inch turn to the right and the
ball would have run in towards the hole, probably finishing dead.
The ball, however, veered as it ran along the top of the hazard,
hung for a moment and then dropped into the sand. That has happened countless times before and will happen at this road hole
many times again.

Bruen was obviously dismayed. He stepped into the bunker,
hit a big explosion shot and the ball struck the top of the bunker,
and rolled back. He was now playing 5. He blasted out with his second attempt and holed in two putts. This meant it was a 7 ...
Bruen's figures were: In – 3, 3, 4, 4, 5, 4, 4, 7, 4 = 38. Total 75.

He was now five strokes behind the leaders, with two rounds to
play. On the last day of the Open, Jimmy took another 75 and a

76 and, of course, did not win. It seems that some loss of putting touch in the morning and a disastrous 9 at the sixth in the afternoon made all the difference.

On the very first hole in the morning it seems that Jimmy misjudged an approach putt and went 5 feet past and missed the one back. This probably upset his confidence, but he appeared to have recovered with two powerful wood shots to the fifth and a 2-yards putt, he had a birdie 4, but dropped another shot at the sixth after being bunkered off the tee and, going right through the eighth which is a par 3 hole, he again dropped another shot to take 38 to the turn. But a 5-yard putt for a 3 at the tenth and a 2-yard putt at the eleventh for a 2 put him right back in the game.

At the twelfth, Bruen, after driving to within 30 yards of the green, played a pitch and run badly and had to be content with a 4. With a further three putts from 5 yards at the thirteenth he dropped another shot.

The seventeenth had been somewhat of a 'Waterloo' for Bruen on the previous days. This time he seemed to have it beaten and he was on the green 5 yards from the pin in 3 shots but he required three putts to get down and a 4 at the last gave him a 75.

In the last round in the afternoon Jimmy again three-putted the first hole. He lost another stroke to par at the fourth and then real disaster struck him at the sixth. This hole is fringed by whins. His drive finished in the vast tangle of whins, holing out finally in 9. This put him seven over 4s and his score looked like going up into the 80s. However, Jimmy was still to play some fantastic golf. He played the next seven holes in five under 4s with figures from the eighth reading 3, 2, 4, 4, 3, 4, 3 and, although he dropped another shot at the fifteenth, he finished in 4, 4, 3 for a round of 76.

The result was, of course, somewhat disappointing, but what amateur golfer aged nineteen would not give his right arm to win the Best Amateur prize in the Open Championship finishing only eight strokes behind the winner? The comparison of the scores of the leaders with the two qualifying rounds included may be of interest. Scores for the six rounds and the totals are as follows: J. Bulla – 71, 72, 77, 71, 71, 73 = 435; J. Bruen – 69, 69, 72, 75, 75, 76 = 436; R. Whitcombe – 72, 72, 71, 75, 74, 74 = 438; P. Alliss – 71, 72, 75, 73, 74, 74 = 439; J. Fallon – 71, 75, 71, 73, 71, 79

= 440; M. Pose – 73, 72, 71, 72, 76, 76 = 440; A. Perry – 74, 75, 71, 74, 73, 76 = 443; A. D. Locke – 73, 74, 70, 75, 76, 75 = 443; R. Burton (the winner) – 78, 76, 70, 72, 77, 71 = 444; W. E. Kenyon – 76, 76, 73, 75, 74, 74 = 448; S. L. King – 79, 75, 74, 72, 75, 73 = 448; D. J. Rees – 76, 75, 71, 74, 75, 77 = 448.

If, then, the qualifying scores had been counted, Jimmy Bruen would have been second in the Open and the eventual winner. Dick Burton would only have finished ninth.

10

66 ON NEWCASTLE

Jimmy Bruen had now, of course, established himself amongst the world's greatest golfers, professional or amateur, and much was to be written about him after his performance in the Open at St Andrew's. In the *Sunday Express* P. B. (Laddie) Lucas wrote:

> At the risk of having a shower of controversy poured on my head I make bold to say that Bruen was the best player in the field.
>
> In three years time he will, I believe, be standing out in golf as emphatically as Bobby Jones did in his day. Furthermore, I make this prophecy – he will win the Open before he wins the Amateur Championship. Yes, yes I know you think I am exaggerating and all the rest of it … Alex Kyle, the Amateur champion, made a very sound remark when he said 'You know you go home with these tales about Bruen and no one ever believes them, but they are true right enough'.
>
> You can't say why he is so good. It is nature, of course. But what the boys do think is that he has a more acute sense of distance than anyone else playing golf. Whatever it is Bruen now stands alone, wonderfully alone, and it is only a question of time before the golfing world is at his feet.

In an article in *The People* of Sunday, 9 July, 'McTavish' says:

> Some folk thought that Bruen was just one of the many boys who could do wonders at an early age and that he would soon be forgotten. Indeed so sceptical were some of the professionals that they predicted in his first Open he would never be among the challengers, but this boy Bruen has proved that nothing can shake him. In his opening qualifying round he returned a 69 on the old course despite the most unpromising opening, for he had two 6s in his first few holes.
>
> But the Irishman is made of real golfing stuff, for he was able to get those bad holes out of his mind and go on to make the first record for the extended old course.

Yet another article by somebody with the *nom de plume*, 'Caletee' stated:

Jimmy Bruen, Éire's meteoric young golfer, is one of the games phenomena. St Andrew's has clinched that point. Amateur parallels of his pinnacle of skill at his age do not take long to list. John Ball finished sixth in an old-time Open when he was fifteen but outside that the quotable instances number but three. Francis Quiet beat Vardan and Ray after a famous tie and Bobby Jones won the Championship of the Southern States of America when he was seventeen. Getting into the professional side, young Tommy Morris won the Open Championship for the first time in his twentieth year. As a shot-maker Bruen is wonderful, but what sticks out a mile about him is his quite extraordinary mentality for big occasion golf. Boys in boys' events parade a certain confidence, but most youngsters just turned nineteen would be completely out of their depth amongst the cream of the professional world. But not Bruen.

In that more than anything else he is the amazing exception, the genius the game throws up only once in a blue moon.

… Bruen combines Ryder Cup efficiency with a mature confidence of a seasoned campaigner and these are the factors that make him different.

Before he took the tee for his second qualifying round last week they were chafing him in his hotel about the difficulty of keeping it up. But Bruen laughed at them and told them in a normal casual way that he would break 70 again. And he did. This Irish lad is phenomena and enigma in one … in the past two years not a player in the world, professional or amateur, has hit the ball so consistently well, week in and week out ...

In my experience of big golf I have never seen anything to justify the description of a shot production machine more than the Bruen golf.

When he crosses the Atlantic next year with the Walker Cup expedition, I fancy he will take America by storm. The scribes will think up all sorts of wise cracks about his style, but I think he will clean up their national championship.

At the moment his thoughts run better in score than matchplay but the highest matchplay honours can hardly escape his steamroller golf, if he can keep it going … nothing that Bruen does in the way of brilliance any longer surprises anybody.

After a week's rest, James Bruen went to Newcastle for the Irish Open Championship which once again he was not to win, but as always he hit the headlines, this time with a record breaking 66 in the first round. This round is well described in *The Irish Times* of 19 July:

James Bruen again struck the high spots in the first round of the
Open Championship of Ireland which began today at the links,
Royal County Down Club with a magnificent 66 which set a record
for the extended course. He was the central figure of some splendid scoring ... he held his place throughout the long day but close
on his heels came the Irish professional champion, Paddy Mahon
of Royal Dublin with a 68 ...

The last time the Championship was played here in 1935 Burt
Gadd set a record for the course with 66 but the links then was 299
yards shorter than the present one which measures 6,833 yards ...

... in his second successive national championship Bruen has
set a very hot pace for the field, and I am firmly convinced that he
will keep it up, and that he is nicely set for the championship which
has not yet been won by an amateur. Unlike the Open Championship every round will count in this one, which is, from Bruen's
point of view, much more satisfactory than were the conditions of
St Andrew's when his two qualifying rounds of 69 did not come
into the final reckoning.

The weather when the first pair drove off was ideal with no
wind or rain, but the downpour of Monday night slowed down the
fairways and greens considerably, so that it was playing to every
yard of its length. When Bruen began by taking three putts on the
fourth green it looked ominous, but it was only a momentary lapse
and, from that on, his play on the green was really magnificent. On
the holes out he required only fifteen putts and homeward he took
but fourteen – only twenty-nine in all ...

His powers of recovery when he did stray a little were exem-
plified at the second hole. There he cut his drive, was then bunkered, chipped out and got down in one putt. The third is 450 yards
long and on in two he holed from about 5 yards for a 3 which blot-
ted out completely that opening lapse. He, however, dropped a
stroke at the short fourth. 10 yards short from the tee he hit the flag
with his second but missed for a 3 from 5 feet. Thereafter, everything went splendidly for the Cork lad ... for an outward score of
34.

He started home with 3, 4, 4 having one putt at the 495-yards
twelfth. A great sequence of 3s – four in a row – followed ... He
almost had a 2 at the short fourteenth. The 407-yards fifteenth is
uphill but a drive and a No. 7 iron got him home and from 5 yards
he holed another putt.

... His 4 at the seventeenth was another illustration of his wonderful powers of recovery whenever he does get into trouble, which
is so seldom. The tee shot was cut a bit and he had to play from
heavy rough but he took an iron, went for the green, carried the

bunker on the right, and hole high he made certain of his 4s. That left him to get a 4 for a 65 but a second to the home hole was sliced a little and he had to pitch over the bunker (Note: this hole is 530 yards long). That, however, did not trouble him and, going for his 4 with his putt, he just failed. He had eight 3s and only two 5s. This record-breaking round still stands and it is believed in Newcastle that it will probably never be broken. His card read: Out – 5, 4, 3, 4, 4, 4, 3, 3, 4 = 34 and Home 3, 4, 4, 3, 3, 3, 3, 4, 5 = 32 for his second nine, total 66.

After that round Jimmy received a telegram which read: 'Glad I am not there. Go on handing it out. Terrific stuff' signed Henry Cotton.

In the second round Bruen did not play well and F. J. C. Pignon in the *Daily Mail* wrote:

The desperate efforts of nearly 100 professionals failed in their attempts to catch James Bruen ... Bruen still holds a slender lead over the whole field with an aggregate of 140. Today the Irish youth entertained a big and enthusiastic crowd by playing less like an automaton, making some very human errors and eventually went around in 74.

Bruen is now one stroke in front of Arthur Lees, the Yorkshire player who returned 72 today ...

Bruen had opened the door to his colleagues by playing some wayward second shots. He is one of the finest iron club players in the country, but today he was not impressive with these shots. Had he not putted so well – he took only fourteen putts during his outward half of 36 – Bruen might have lost his lead.

He holed a 10-yarder for a 3 at the third, the longest putt that he holed, and he ran down about half a dozen putts of between 5 and 10 feet during the round.

On the other hand, he missed three quite holable putts. But through the green Bruen had to do some recovery work and he did it excellently. He did not have a single 3 on his homeward half of 38 ... At the tenth he played a wild tee shot. At the fourteenth he missed the green and failed with a 2-yard putt and he was unlucky at the sixteenth. The hole is 267 yards and Bruen was just short of the green with his tee shot, played off a twig, the ball finished over the green and so close to a fence that he could hardly swing his club. This series of misfortunes ended with a 5 for this hole. Bruen was not satisfied with a round of nearly one stroke better than the scratch score but it was too good for most of his rivals.

On the last day of that championship Bruen did not play well, taking 75 and 81. Throughout the day he was the outstanding attraction, nevertheless, and even when in the evening he took 41 for the homeward holes, the mass of spectators remained loyally with him.

In spite of that bad last round of 81 he still, of course, won the Best Amateur prize and finished sixth in the Championship only being beaten by Arthur Lees, Reg Whitcombe, Bobby Locke, G. M. White and Fred Daly. The leaders with their four rounds were: A. Lees 69, 72, 74, 72 = 287; R. Whitcombe 76, 69, 72, 72 = 289; G. M. White 69, 76, 73, 74 = 292; F. Daly 72, 71, 77, 74 = 294; J. Bruen Jnr 66, 74, 75, 81 = 296; M. Faulkner 74, 75, 75, 73 = 297; C. H. Ward 75, 77, 73, 72 = 297; A. Bradshaw 75, 72, 74, 76 = 297; W. J. Branch 73, 77, 73, 74 = 297; J. Fallon 74, 72, 76, 76 = 298. The next best amateur to Bruen was J. B. Carr with a total of 306.

11

THE WAR YEARS

On 3 September 1939 the Second World War broke out and while Jimmy Bruen was to continue playing golf, he was not to hit the headlines for another seven years. A tremendous gap in any golfer's playing career, and who is to guess how many championships he would have won had the war not taken place and championship golf continued?

In those days I remember playing quite a lot of golf with James Bruen during the holiday period from school when I was just a boy. I remember also his efforts to get the kink out of his swing and I don't think he ever really succeeded. He did at one stage virtually iron it out completely but I think his golf began to suffer and, after not a very long time, he went back again to his own original method, with the loop probably more pronounced than ever. Around that time a nice little piece appeared written by George Allison in the *Sunday Express*:

> People often ask me about Jimmy Bruen. And my answer is that he is an unusually nice fellow considering he's had enough publicity to swell the heads of a regiment of golfers, and that if the war is not a fatal interruption in his career he will be the greatest golfer we have ever known. Wait and see.

In 1942, Louis T. Stanley, writing in *The Field* under the heading, 'Two golfers who are reasonably certain of lasting recognition', wrote:

> There is a golfer who although a mere youth can, by virtue of what he has already accomplished, be reasonably certain of lasting recognition. That player is nineteen-year-old James Bruen. I remember watching him at Birkdale in 1936 when he became the first winner for Ireland of the Boys' Amateur Championship and the manner of his overwhelming victory over William Innes by 11 and 9 showed that he held considerable promise, although few dreamed that it would come to fruition with such rapidity.
>
> At the outset of his career, among his elders he was treated with a certain amount of criticism, inevitable if you do well in this life, and which, provided you possess a lively sense of humour, can

be taken as a compliment. In Bruen's case the trouble lay partly in an excessive confidence in his ability to beat all comers irrespective of their age or reputation – a task which few would regard as a failing and which many of his would-be detractors sadly lacked. It was truly amazing to see this so developed in a boy of such tender years, and what was even more refreshing was the decisive way he translated it into action, much to the embarrassment of some who started intending to patronise.

The climax came during the trial matches at St Andrew's prior to the Walker Cup match ... I expected him to win the Amateur Championship, a prophecy that appeared to be well on the way to fulfilment when a giant killer [the Second World War] arose and closed his hooks. I am certain, however, that his time will come; in fact, given reasonable luck, he should win the Amateur title more than once ... Time alone will show when championship days return. In the interim it is to be hoped that his enforced absence from major golf will not tame his spirit ... My own observations would tend to prove ... mainly that the greatest players have been those most nervous and highly strung. Not that I am advocating losing one's temper in order to become a good golfer but a certain amount of untamed spirit must be infused into one's game....

After 1939 Jimmy naturally had to settle down and start making a living for himself. He was keen at this stage to join either the Irish or British army but did not do so because of strong pressure from his family. His first job was in a large textile factory in Cork but I don't think this ever really appealed to him. He seemed to be attracted to the insurance world.

In 1942, while he was working for an Irish insurance company in Tralee, Co. Kerry, Jimmy used to cycle from Tralee to Cork quite regularly – a distance of about 70 miles. On one of these occasions the weather was very bad and Jimmy stopped off in Killarney where he met a few of his friends and stood in the rain talking golf. By the time he got home to Cork he was extremely ill and was running a very high temperature. Apparently he did not say anything to his parents and failed to change his wet clothes. The following morning he was very sick indeed and, in fact, for quite some time he was completely paralysed.

He and Nell were engaged at this time, and she came down to Cork to care for him. According to her, he could not even lift his head. Nell's father, who was an eminent doctor and had now become a great friend of the Bruen family, also came down to see if he could help Jimmy. Apparently he pumped him with M & B, at the time the latest drug. After a time, Jimmy recovered, but got up too soon and suffered a relapse. Eventually, after a long rest, he recovered completely. In hindsight, Nell, however, believed that he probably had rheumatic fever – although the illness at the time was never named – and that it could also have contributed to his early death, from a heart attack.

Nevertheless he was soon back again on the golf course, as well as working hard at starting his new business as an insurance broker. All these years he was to have some remarkable scores at Cork Golf Club. For example, his club record for the years 1937–43 for forty-seven rounds of that course worked out at 100 under 4s. These figures were in the competition book at the club but were unfortunately destroyed in a fire in 1946. In 1937–40 he scored 70s to 74s with the greatest of ease playing off +2, and had the occasional 67, 68 and 69. However, his gross figures for 1941 (he was then playing off +4) for fifteen rounds of medal play against par, all holed out but not including stableford, included 64, 66, 68 (four times) 69 (six times).

In all he had played nineteen rounds in the 60s, again the stableford scores excluded. His lowest score of 64 was in a stroke competition on 17 March 1942. In 1943 for nineteen rounds in competitions during the winter period, October to April, he was 73 under 4s and seventeen of those rounds read as follows: 71, 66, 70, 68, 69, 65, 67, 70, 65, 69, 65, 70, 73, 65, 69, 73, 67. In that year he also won the president's prize at both Muskerry and Cork golf clubs off +4 handicap. At this stage too he was the holder of seven course records. They included Portmarnock 70, Newcastle 66, Royal Portrush 71, Baltray 71, Cork Golf Club 67, Muskerry 65 and Macroom 67.

Other than the Cork Scratch Cup in 1940 and 1941, which he won again for the third and fourth times in a row, Jimmy played no other top class golf. He did, however, play many exhibition matches for the Red Cross. In the 1940 Scratch Cup in Cork he waltzed, as usual, into the final where he met Arthur Dinan another scratch handicap golfer from Cork Golf Club. In the first round in the final Jimmy went around the course in 69, and was in fact only 4 up as Dinan had gone round in 73. Both were out in 34 in the first nine holes and Bruen was back in 35 to Dinan's 39. In the afternoon the first two holes were halved and then

Dinan began to play indifferent shots and lost the next four to be 8 down, Bruen finally winning the match 8 and 6.

In the 1941 final Bruen met H. F. Cronin, a former Irish lawn tennis international. Cronin, a 4 handicap player, could not possibly hope to give the holder a close match. As it was, he was able, with the assistance of some fine putts, to stem the tide for a goodly portion of the morning round, but a bad collapse cost him the last three holes in a row, and he was 9 down when they went to lunch. After that it was only a matter of time and, having made a mess of the twenty-second hole, Cronin lost the next three for the match. Bruen played devastatingly steady golf, finally winning by 13 and 11.

I notice from a cutting in *The Irish Times* of Wednesday, 11 June 1941 a small paragraph headed 'A 65 by Bruen at Dollymount'. The paragraph goes on: 'Playing with machine-like accuracy at Dollymount (Royal Dublin Golf Club) yesterday James Bruen holed out in 65. His golf was more brilliant than ever. And not once was he off the fairway'.

I also found another interesting *Irish Times* article of around that period written by the late P. J. Rooney, well-known Irish golf writer. He is writing about who was the most 'picturesque' figure in Irish amateur golf for the twenty years prior to the war. Why he uses the word 'picturesque', as opposed to 'great' or 'colourful', I am not quite sure but I must presume that by 'picturesque' he means spectacular. In any case, the article goes on to say:

> The question has often been debated in club circles and asked by writers of the game, and naturally present-day golfers have no doubt as to who is entitled to the distinction. From the day he became Boys' Champion James Bruen has rightly been looked upon as the most remarkable figure not only in Irish golf but also in British amateur golf. If any doubt of this point did exist so far as British golf is concerned it was disputed by Mr Leonard Crawley in his recently published article in *Golf Monthly* in which he expressed the hope that when the Open Championship is revised the Irishman will 'gain the honour to which his prowess as a golfer entitles him'. In point of fact it is extremely doubtful if any Irish amateur golfer would attain the eminence to which in a few years Bruen ascended in competition with the greatest of golfers, British and American, amateur and professional.
>
> A very debatable point, however, would be the question: 'Who would you rank next to James Bruen?' One recalls such names as

Lionel Munn, Major G. N. C. Martin, Major Charles Heslett, Edward Spiller, Dr J. D. MacCormack, John Burke, Cecil Ewing, Joe Brown, the brothers Frank and Roy McConnell, Michael Crowley and Dr Gerry Owens. [Of course at that stage the great Joe Carr had not reached the pinnacle which he was to reach in later years.]

In the autumn of 1943 Jimmy Bruen married Miss Eleanor Cremin, daughter of Dr and Mrs W. C. Cremin of St Stephen's Green, Dublin. Nell was, of course, the little girl with whom, many years beforehand in Bundoran, he had played his first round of golf.

Jimmy and Nell bought a house next to Jimmy's father in Blackrock, Co. Cork, close to the famous Blackrock Castle. This was an old house and Jimmy with his usual vigour set about modernising it, and building the garden from scratch. Jimmy loved this garden and many years later his friends were to admire his beautiful work which included the inevitable putting green. Looking across the river from his house Jimmy could see part of Cork Golf Club and on many occasions he used to row across the river on fine days to play his golf, as that was a much shorter way than going by road.

Jimmy was always a lover of boats – I suppose all of us who live in Cork are as we live so close to the sea – and it was about this time he took to sailing as a recreation. All this time he was building up his business practice as an insurance broker and was, I think, the second broker to go into that business in the city. In those days it was a one-man business and took up a tremendous amount of his time, but hard work was never something that Jimmy shirked, whether it was on the golf course, in his business in his garden or indeed anywhere else. And while he kept his hand in playing club golf he did not play in any of the larger tournaments. Just after the war a golf writer in an Irish newspaper summed it up well, I think, when he wrote:

Since the announcement of the resumption of international golf and the big championship events everyone is asking where is Jimmy Bruen, the 'boy wonder' of 1936, the number one player on the first victorious team against America in the Walker Cup in 1938 and the number one amateur in the British Open Championship in 1939. This golfing wizard, easily the greatest we have ever produced in Ireland, disappeared as into thin air shortly after the outbreak of war, and has not pitted his skill against the top ranking players since. But Bruen is still playing. He is still in the top rank and it is a certainty that he will be in the Irish team in the coming international tournament against England, Scotland and Wales. Bruen suffered a severe illness in the early days of the war and this necessitated him giving up the game altogether for a while, but he has been back for some time now and some of the scores he is putting up are reminiscent of the old Bruen at his best.

Regularly he goes around his home course at Little Island in the low 60s and during a recent visit to Dublin he has been trying himself out in private games over the testing Portmarnock and Royal Dublin courses. He recently had a practice at Royal Dublin and returned an amazing 68 despite missing two comparatively easy putts. This score equals the amateur score for the course and is only two shots outside the score set up by Charles Whitcombe, the English Ryder Cup player.

Lack of intense practice in which he used to indulge in pre-war days have left few marks on Bruen's game. He is still getting tremendous distances into his drive and it is only on the greens, where he has lost some of his old amazing skill, that he shows the effects of a long lay-off from competitive golf. That he is rapidly coming back to his best is certain and equally so is the fact that he will be a power and an attraction at the coming big tournaments.

I would disagree with the golf writer when he said that Jimmy had lost some of his old amazing skill at putting, for whatever part of Jimmy's game had its ups and downs, I have always felt that his putting never deteriorated at all, right up to his death.

12

AMATEUR CHAMPION 1946

In 1946 the British Amateur Championship was revived after the war and Jimmy entered. His very entry caused excitement, and many golf correspondents started writing him up before he left home at all. In fact, in a small paragraph in one newspaper it was even reported that 'Bruen left Dublin yesterday on his way to Birkdale'. Another correspondent writing in the *Dublin Evening Mail* (alas, no longer with us), wrote:

> The stir which the announcement of Jimmy Bruen's return to big golf has made is particularly hard on those many fine players who have done so much to keep the game going – as far as big competitions are concerned – during the past six years. But I think that even they will readily admit that they are only in the halfpenny place, so as to speak, when compared to a man who must now be termed the ex-Boy Wonder.
>
> Bruen in a short few years made a name for himself which I feel sure would have lived for many decades even if he had not entered for another competition. He was a wonder – he was more than a wonder, he was the miracle player of the years preceding the war. It is a far throw from golf to boxing but I know or knew of no sportsman in the years immediately preceding the war whose name slipped off the tongues of the general public as easily as did Jimmy Bruen's, with the exception of the fistic exponents in the heavier grade such as Joe Lewis and, of course, our own Jack Doyle. For a golfer to hold such prominence in the minds of a sporting and general public is really remarkable and it would take a name of quite outstanding ability to do so.
>
> Well Bruen was more than that. He was the talk everywhere the game of golf is played and if, as seemed likely at one stage, he had turned professional and gone on tour with some of the big noises of the game – an opportunity which was offered to him – he would probably have made more money than any other man at the game ever before him. But Jimmy decided to retain his amateur status and then the war came along to cheat him of an opportunity of showing his powers and for the past six years he has lain fallow, so to speak. As is the case with all men as prominent as Bruen, rumour was always ripe about him. He was ill shortly after the war started

and dame rumour said he would never be able to play again. He did play again and by all accounts as well as ever. Then the never idle dame said that he would never again take part in big competitions and the fact that he missed out the minor Irish championships gave support to the rumour. But the announcement that he has entered for the British Open Amateur Championship at Birkdale at the end of the month has scotched all rumours.

It is interesting to note that Bruen and Birkdale are no strangers. Birkdale, which has only just come into the championship rota in England, is one of the most luxurious clubs there. Its clubhouse is a cross between a super cinema and a modern airport and its course is said to be far and away ahead of such tradition-steeped spots as St Andrew's. But its connection with Bruen or vice versa, well, it was there that he put his foot on the first rung of the ladder of fame way back in 1936 when he 'blitzed' the opposition in the Boys' Championship.

How is he going to fare this time when the opposition is all that is best in the amateur ranks? No one can tell. If he is the Bruen of old he should win; but it is a bit early yet to discuss the prospects.

I remember well playing with him a few days before he went to that championship. His golf was simply superb, but he seemed to have developed a strange reluctance for top competition and, in fact, had not quite made up his mind that he was going to go at all. I do not claim to have influenced his decision on that occasion, but I remember saying to him, 'Why not Jimmy, as I don't think anyone will be able to beat you'. As we sat in the sun outside Cork Golf Club discussing the matter, his old mentor, Jack Higgins, approached us and, when Jimmy again expressed his reluctance, Jack got quite edgy saying, 'I want the Amateur champion in this club'. I began to suspect that day that he was, in fact, a reluctant hero.

From the word go, Jimmy was, of course, the favourite and he was drawn in the top half of the draw, the same section as Alec Kyle, the Scot and last winner of the title in 1939, and who also defeated Jimmy in that championship. It was the first time too that Frank Stranahan from the United States had appeared on the British golf scene and, interestingly enough, he was to play John Beck, the captain of the 1938 British Walker Cup team, in the first round. Also, it was the first time in the history of golf that the wireless was used to control the crowd. Four sets of apparatus operating over a 5-mile radius were installed in various parts of the course, with the main station at the clubhouse.

In the second round Jimmy played Albert Margolles of North Middlesex whom he defeated on the eleventh green by 9 and 7, but it was not so much the margin of his victory as the way in which he achieved it that impressed. Henry Longhurst wrote:

> He was driving the ball a thoroughly colossal distance and some of his shots were a constant source of conversation in the clubhouse afterwards. Those who had seen him were to be found searching new audiences to whom they might retell their story.
>
> For example, the first hole is 450 yards long and the normal golfer plays to the right of a large hump on the left of the fairway. Bruen not only carried the hump but finished no more than 100 yards from the flag. From here he pitched up and holed his putt for a 3. Then again at the tenth, 390 yards and a dog leg to the left, Bruen, taking a wider line than any that could be conceived possible, carried the whole of the intervening sand-hills and finished 10 yards short of the green – a really monstrous stroke.
>
> What was so invigorating for the spectators about Bruen's play is that while so many of the players after seven years absence from the big golf have a timid air of uncertainly about their game, he seems to be attacking all the time. Henry Cotton remarked to me today that in his whole experience of golf he had never seen anyone who got such acceleration into the club head just before the moment of impact. Cotton in fact rates Bruen in the very highest class and so indeed do all who have seen him here. Anything can happen in an 18-hole knock-out championship but my own impression is that the American Frank Stranahan and Leonard Crawley are the only two who are to be classed with Bruen.
>
> … Birkdale, 6,730 yards long with more than 2,000 yards of walking between the greens and tees is essentially a strong man's course and one for a man who can drive hard and straight. From this point of view Bruen more than adequately fits the bill and if he wins there will hardly be a man who will not say, 'The best man won'.

In the third round Bruen was a late starter against his English opponent, W. J. B. Giradet, a lusty golfer in the early 1930s. Bruen in the long game was a complete master but Giradet, untroubled by a large gallery, put up a fine show and was only beaten by 2 and 1. Bruen was fortunate in his late start as he missed a heavy rain storm and went on in almost summer-like conditions.

On the Thursday of that week the morning matches, though

good, were but a prelude to the afternoon's. Bruen was most doggedly hunted by a young Scottish golfer, J. Prestley of Fraserburgh, who utterly refused to be frightened and played extremely well. Bruen was around in 74 and won on the last green by one hole.

Now for the afternoon. Bruen played Charlie Stowe of Penn. The golfing correspondent of *The Times* wrote:

> ... a delightful match, delightfully played, a perfect model for the potterers and time-wasters to imitate. For seven holes Bruen was tremendous and overwhelming. It was not so much the fact that he holed them in twenty-six shots. It was the kind of golf which must have been heartbreaking to play against. Stowe played very well but he was being perceptively outplayed and he was 2 down, as well he might be. Then Bruen had a shortage putt for a 4 to be 3 up at the eighth. He just missed it and both players seemed to sense that a chance had been lost and a crisis was past.
>
> Bruen began to be erratic and to play loose long iron shots – always his weak point. Stowe ... leapt ... like a tiger, and from 2 down at the turn became 1 up at the thirteenth. Bruen hung on. Both had putts for 2 at the seventeenth and both missed, and Stowe was still 1 up coming to the last hole. He laid a little run up dead in 3. Bruen laid another still more dead and what was more it was a dead stymie. Stowe got the loft but failed at the line and out they must go again for Stowe to take three putts and Bruen win in a 4 at the nineteenth.

This was a lucky break for Jimmy but then, who ever won a championship without a lucky break?

Bruen's next victim in the quarter-final and semi-final were Bill Tweddle, former champion and Harry Walker, former Cheshire title holder. He had a great tussle before disposing of Tweddle who was in brilliant form with his wooden putter. All square with four to play, Bruen, after losing the fifteenth, took the next two holes and he got an easy half at the last for a one-hole victory. There was a lot of good golf in the match and Tweddle putted well but Bruen used his hard-hitting prowess to the best possible advantage. Early on, the Corkman played superbly on and around the greens. At the turn they were square, each being 35. Fortunes fluctuated until they were level with four holes to play. After losing the fifteenth, Bruen had great wins at the sixteenth and seventeenth and victory came on the last green with a confident 4 against which Tweddle could do no better than equal.

Walker made a good fight of it, 3 down after four holes. However, Bruen was a millstone around his neck and though he got Bruen down to 2 he was eventually beaten 3 and 2. Bruen ended the match level 4s, great golf in atrocious weather conditions. He finished without his favoured mashie niblick. The head of the club flew off as he played a shot to the tenth green. So bad were the conditions that few spectators braved the elements.

Again quoting *The Times*:

> Bruen at first looked like running away from Walker who began very shakily. He was 3 up after five holes but at that point Walker hung on manfully. He was severely out-driven for Bruen's length is really prodigious, but he twice got his man down to 2 and never ceased to chase him. Bruen made one or two loose iron shots as seemed inevitable, but on the whole it was a masterful and impressive display.

And so the stage was set for a final in which James Bruen met Robert Sweeney, of the Royal and Ancient. Bob Sweeney, aged thirty-three, son of an American financier was a well-known golfer on this side of the Atlantic. He graduated from Oxford with his brother, Charles, and during the war first served with the American Eagle Squadron and later became a captain of an RAF liberator bomber. On the way to the final Bruen had been taken to the home green three times and Sweeney had twice been to the nineteenth and once to the twentieth, further demonstrating the point that it takes just that little bit of extra luck to get through a championship – but somehow it always seems to go with the better players.

For a description of the final, I think that none could be better than that of Henry Longhurst writing in the *Irish Independent*:

> The victory of James Bruen over Robert Sweeney by four and three in the 36-hole final of the British Amateur Championship at Birkdale near Southport made him the first Irishman to win the title. He was, if I may so so, a most popular winner. People like him for the fact that he played so well without giving himself airs and graces and to the spectator, of course, he is full value for money ...
>
> A final at Southport can often be more like Derby Day than a golf match but a strong west wind on Saturday, with a hint of showers to come, confined the gallery mostly to persons familiar

with the game and it was possible with a little ingenuity to see every shot. How well worth seeing it all was! Sweeney, who won the title in a very imposing way at Sandwich in 1937, is still a most attractive stylist and … a long and powerful player. Sweeney started rather unfortunately and Bruen drove on to some mounds across the left of the fairway, which even he couldn't carry and then played into a bunker beside the green. Sweeney with a fine drive took too short a club for his second and saw it fade not only into a bunker, which the right club would have carried, but also plug itself high up in the sand. He took 6 and was 1 down when he might have been 1 up.

There was a good deal of exchanging of holes until the end of the seventh where Bruen was again 1 up, though Sweeney had played remarkably fewer bad shots. Then they settled down to the real championship stuff halving hole after hole at the right figure until the 3 by Sweeney squared the match at the fifteenth.

At the next hole, however, he made the most expensive error. Perhaps with the fear of a stymie in his head he putted short, missed the next and lost the hole. Bruen leaped on him with a 2 at the seventeenth and went into lunch 2 up. The score was approximately 74 against 76 – rare good going in the conditions – but there is no doubt about it, Bruen was a bit lucky in this round. The eleventh was the first hole where he hit a drive onto the fairway (to say nothing of one or two second shots) yet he was able, partly through his own sheer strength it is true, to get away with it every time. If it had been one of his unlucky days his ball might five times have been almost unplayable in the tough scrub, characteristic of Birkdale. At the eighth hacking his ball out of it he broke his mashie niblick, or rather, Gordon Peters' mashie niblick which he had borrowed to replace his own broken in the rough on the previous day.

It was again a terrific piece of good fortune to find Henry Cotton walking in the crowd using an identical club as a walking stick, and at the very next hole he hit a superb shot with it. In the afternoon with the rain coming down in torrents, Sweeney won the first hole which was encouraging but ran into a really bad patch for the next three.

Then at the fifth Bruen put in the first of two really shattering blows. He was just off the green in 2 with Sweeney lying 4 yards away with an obvious chance of a 3. In went Bruen's, Sweeney's did not, and what a lot of difference there is between 1 down and 3 down. Then at the eighth Bruen went and did it again – this time from about 15 yards. Sweeney hung on and got a hole back, but the long fourteenth really settled it.

With two shots delivered against the wind and rain-sodden

ground Bruen carried 520 yards. I should not have believed it if I
had not seen it … and resultant 4 made him dormie. Sweeney, who
has played with Jimmy Thompson, Sam Sneed and all the long hit-
ters in the United States, declared that none of them could have
come anywhere near equalling those two prodigious strokes. So
this immensely satisfactory final played between two fine players
on a fine course and at the right pace ended at the thirty-third hole,
and the general opinion was that the right man had won and hats
off to the loser.

So, at the age of twenty-six, Jimmy Bruen, with a score of one
over fours for the final, had won the British Amateur Championship and Jack Higgins did indeed have the Amateur champion
in Cork Golf Club.

When Jimmy was presented with the cup by F. D. B. Hill,
captain of Birkdale, he told the hundreds of enthusiasts who had
waited half an hour in heavy rain for the ceremony, 'This is what
I have always dreamed of, to take this back to Ireland. It has been
my life's ambition'.

It was a case of 'third time lucky', as he himself expressed it.
After this, more thousands of words were to be written about
Jimmy Bruen, and some, I think, are well worth quoting. I par-
ticularly like an article written by Sam McKinlay in the *Scottish
Field* of July 1946 under the heading 'Portrait of a Champion':

> It is inevitable that James Bruen, the Amateur golf champion, should
> be called 'the bear' and he has the strength and solidity of that ani-
> mal, as well as a kindred name. But it would be a great mistake to
> think, as many still do, that he is a 'grisly bear'. The errors that men
> make when they are young live after them….
>
> … Bruen is to this day associated with some excessive exuber-
> ance when he was a boy playing in his first Amateur Champion-
> ship, and although he was not to blame his early reputation suf-
> fered. The Bruen who is the first post-war Amateur champion is a
> grown man, a great golfer and a very charming and pleasant per-
> son indeed. He is also, behind this façade of seeming imperturba-
> bility and grim concentration, a very human individual, a prey like
> lesser golfing mortals to the hopes, fears and aspirations that traf-
> fic on the links arouses.
>
> I feel I can speak with authority on Bruen because I had the
> good fortune to be his personal steward during the final of the
> Amateur Championship at Birkdale….
>
> There was one revealing moment at the end of the game.

Bruen, dormie 4, was lying dead in three shots and Sweeney was still off the green in the like. Short of a miracle, the match and the Championship were Bruen's. He huddled under my umbrella and said, 'This is the happiest moment of my life', and although millions have spoken that sentence, the young Irishman spoke with a fervour that gave the words new currency. I must confess that I shared the joy because he had played superbly … he was the best player in the great field of 263 and it would have been an indictment of the Championship conditions if he had not won.

But, say the critics, was he not specially lucky in the finals to find good lies from tee shots? Should a champion be able to drive straighter than Bruen? Did he not save his neck with brilliant recoveries and good putting? I concede some of these points but there is one reservation I must make.

Bruen hit the ball so far that the Birkdale course was more difficult for him than for almost anyone else in the field. It is a very fine course but it has one characteristic that troubled Bruen. Half of the holes are dog-legged and the bend of the dog-leg was usually just where a good drive would finish. Bruen, on the other hand, could invariably hit the ball past the angle, so that he had either to swing his shot to the desired spot or make a very bold carry over evil country to find a haven. His landing area was therefore restricted and, unless he hit his shot perfectly, he over-ran the fairway and found trouble. That he was able to extricate himself without disaster was a tribute alike to his strength and his skill….

… two shots that Bruen played in the closing stages of the final were described by Cotton and L. Crawley ... as being the best they have ever seen and beyond the power and skill of any other player known to them.

Some day he will hit all his shots only as he can hit them and the world will wonder anew

Jimmy was interviewed by the golf correspondent of the *Cork Examiner* when he arrived back in Dublin:

In the quiet of his father-in-law's surgery in St Stephen's Green yesterday morning I talked golf for half an hour with Jimmy Bruen. Unknown to all but his family and myself, he had slipped into Dublin with the dawn, fresh from the greatest triumph ever achieved by an Irish golfer.

The manner of his return was typical of the young Corkman … The game is more important to him than the honours it brings … Although we were old acquaintances and I had written thousands of words about him during his golfing career, he was disin-

clined to give an interview at first for newspaper purposes. He
capitulated, however, when I reminded him that it would not be
fair to his hosts of friends and admirers back home in Cork that he
should remain silent. 'Well,' he said ruefully, 'what would you like
me to say?' ... I got from him some interesting impressions of his
history-making week. 'You know,' he said, 'you must have luck in
addition to playing good golf in order to win a championship of
this size. I had the luck and I played myself into form.' I queried
this, remembering the Jimmy Bruen who practised morning, noon
and night ...

'It was different this time,' he said, 'as you know I have been
playing little or no competitive golf. When I got to Birkdale I played only two practice rounds and none at all on the Saturday and
Sunday before the championship. If I had practised intensely in the
weeks beforehand I would have only gone stale, and so decided
simply to play myself into form during the championship. I did
strike form second time out and from then on I was all right ... I
remembered the course well since I won the Boy's Championship
there in 1936. There was no change except that there were five or
six back tees and we did not play from them.'

To the question of how the course played he said, 'It was perfect, very long and made more difficult by heavy rain which fell frequently and a high cross wind.' In three matches his ball was plugged in the fairway and each time was unplayable and each time it
meant the loss of the hole. An idea of the length may be gained
from the fact that the shortest hole on the course is 158 yards, and
each time Bruen played it he had to use a No. 4 iron. Normally for
that distance a mashie niblick would be the club. Another feature is
that for many of the longer holes it was necessary to play for position rather than length, and at those Jimmy had to resort to a No. 1
iron off the tee, thereby losing the advantage of the colossal length
he gets with his wooden club.

Asked how well he played, he answered that he felt quite satisfied at all stages ...

It seems difficult to believe, in view of the post-war absence of
competitive play, that the standard of play in this year's Championship should be better than ever before, but this Bruen told me
was the generally accepted opinion at Birkdale and this was borne
out by no less an authority than Henry Cotton.

Well though he was playing, Bruen had to fight desperately
hard in all but two of his matches, and in the latter stages the only
game in which he felt really comfortable about the result was the
semi-final. His hardest game he felt was in the sixth round when he
had to go to the nineteenth to dispose of Charlie Stowe of Penn.

Next to that was his match against Dr Tweddle who worried him for a long time by sinking phenomenal long putts. In view of the tremendous physical strain involved in the week of match play, I asked Bruen how he got himself fit. 'Well,' he said, 'I spent all my spare time for a couple of weeks before I left chopping down trees and clearing away under-growth at home in Cork and when I got to Birkdale I was as fit as a fiddle.' In spite of this, he added, he felt the strain before the week was out and he was quite tired for the final. In the golfing sense Jimmy had no plans for the immediate future. 'I don't know whether I will play in any more champion-ships this year. I hope to do a lot of sailing and I won't even think of golf for a while.'

... he carried with him another pleasant memory – it was the good sportsmanship of his fellow competitors and the generous applause of the large gallery that followed him on every round. Descending to the vernacular I have no doubt Cork is waiting to shake him by the hand and to say, 'We knew you had it in you, Jimmy'.

It is not often that the subject matter of a leading article on a newspaper is a golfer. However, the week after Jimmy won the Amateur Championship a leading article, part of which I quote, appeared in the *Cork Examiner*:

By his victory in the British Amateur Championship Jimmy Bruen has aroused an enthusiasm and interest in Ireland which penetrates much further than the rank of golfers. His name has been on the lips and in the thoughts of thousands of his fellow countrymen since his victory in the opening rounds and on his success he must be congratulated heartily. From nowhere would he receive more sincere congratulations than the city and county of Cork where he learned and played most of his golf – for he is recognised not only as a great golfer – the best this country has ever produced – but as a great and unassuming sportsman whose new honour, like many he has already won, will attach easily and naturally to him.

... his win will be especially appreciated amongst those who are intimately concerned with the Royal and Ancient game. After seven years of enforced abstention from big golf this young man, who was a mere boy when he led the British Walker Cup team against America in 1937, has shown that all the promise contained in those pre-war performances has been maintained and enhanced ... Those who know James Bruen's game confidently expect that he will rapidly prove himself to have no peer in the modern golfing world ... Congratulations to our new champion. He has touched his

best form in the last round of the final at the end of a gruelling
week. May he go from strength to strength, which is the hallmark
of a champion.

The various club-breaking incidents in this championship of
Jimmy Bruen were well recorded. Henry Cotton himself:

> Bruen broke his No. 7½ [yes, there used to be such a club in those
> days] yesterday and borrowed one from Gordon Peters and broke
> that at the eighth today. I was out following the play using a No. 7½
> of mine to flick off daisy tops and to act as a walking stick, when
> Bruen spotted me and the club. He asked if he could borrow it after
> seeing what it was. The very next shot he used it, playing his sec-
> ond onto the ninth green from a nasty spot with it. I don't know
> what sort of luck that is but it is a good turn of the wheel to say the
> least of it.

Some years later in an interview with Irish sportswriter Jimmy
McGee on the subject of what Jimmy considered the greatest
match of his career – the final of the British Amateur – the matter of the broken club arose again. McGee recalled:

> … then there was a gasp of dismay for as he struck the ball the steel
> shafted club broke and fell from his hand. It was the second club to
> give way under the strain of Bruen's powerful hitting in the cham-
> pionship, but all was well, the ball soared out of the grass and
> reached the green. In the meantime, Bruen was looking anxious for
> he was now short of a much needed 7 iron and as luck would have
> it, there was Henry Cotton strolling through the crowd using a 7 iron
> as a walking stick. In a moment Cotton's club was transferred to
> Bruen's bag and he proceeded to halve the eighth as if nothing had
> happened. Nor was the borrowed club idle for long, for at the ninth
> he found another nasty lie and used it for his second to the green.
>
>   It was a faultless shot and Bruen looked pleased 'Got any
> more like that one?' he said cheerfully to Cotton and got yet anoth-
> er half.

In July of that year an editorial from *Fairway and Hazard* recorded:

> James Bruen of Ireland is the 1946 British Amateur champion and
> a lusty young champion if ever there was one. He is possessed of
> great strength and hits the ball vast distances not only from the
> orthodox places but from the unorthodox places as well. The fact
> that he broke three iron clubs in the week will probably go down
> to posterity. The story embroidered on the way until he becomes a

legendary figure endowed with colossal strength, a giant club breaker! Yet it is not what happened to the club which is the least bit important but what happened to the ball. Bruen's powers of recovery are amazing. It is in part due to his strength that he can burst the ball onto the green out of places from which the average human being would merely emerge thankfully onto the fairway, but at the same time there is an implacable determination and a supreme confidence behind the shot which must supply the motive power to that strength of his. Perhaps therein lies the inch of difference between a fine golfer and a champion. The mental process must come in to tip the balance.

13

THE RELUCTANT HERO

Jimmy Bruen did not play in the Open in 1946, although he had half promised to do so, nor did he play in the Irish Amateur Championship played at Portrush.

He was working very hard at his business. In his own words: 'Business must come before golf'. While there is no doubt that he was very involved in building his business, I do feel that there was something deeper. I felt at the time, as I do now, that the real trouble was that Jimmy had lost his appetite for the rough and tumble and strain of championship golf. He never actually said so – but then Jimmy never said a lot about himself. Nevertheless, I don't really feel that Jimmy Bruen any longer had his heart in golf. He did, of course, make a number of appearances and in-evitably showed that most of his skill was still there, but these were isolated appearances. He was, in fact, a true amateur and even though he practised quite a lot he really was only a week-end golfer from this point on. He took a great interest in the ordi-nary affairs of Cork Golf Club, however, and was captain for two years. Yet I think it's true to say, that fame did not rest too easily on his shoulders and, while the public clamoured for more and more Bruen, he felt that, being an amateur, he should be free to lead his own life.

It was around March in 1947 that he damaged his wrist and in the *Daily Mail* of 10 April he gave his own explanation:

> I was practising hard at hitting the ball well when suddenly my right hand, wrist and fingers and forearm suddenly cracked up. I have no idea how it happened and I certainly never received any injury. This happened about three weeks ago and I have been hop-ing against hope ever since that there will be a change for the better. I was treated by the doctors with penicillin because they thought I might have had blood poisoning. I have been x-rayed twice but the cause is still unknown.
>
> After a final consultation with the doctors I was told my hand must be in plaster for a couple of months.

There is no doubt that he had a very sore right wrist and, in fact, he was given morphine to ease the pain. Nobody will ever find out the real cause of the trouble but Nell Bruen felt that it was the constant strain put on his right hand by his golf swing.

About this time, I was playing with him in a four-ball at Cork Golf Club one day and on the ninth tee, which is a short par 3 hole, when Jimmy hit a stone with the club head. Cork Golf Club is built in a quarry and there are many rocks and stones about. Jimmy was noted in those days for the huge divot he used to take with an iron shot, and on this occasion, with a 9 iron, he took his usual big divot, but his club hit a stone which was concealed under the grass. I remember the club flew out of his hand and he shook his right wrist having got a tremendous jar. I don't know if this was the cause of the trouble but it certainly did not help.

Some years later, Henry Cotton wrote:

> James Bruen, one of the greatest golfing characters of our day, who, as a boy in the pre-war days, was a sensation until he damaged his wrist, is in the hands of a surgeon, getting his wrist operated on. Some bones have been broken and have ossified into a band which in turn used to tear the tendons and generally create a horrible mess, a friend tells me. He is having it operated upon a second time if the first go is not quite right, but it is too early to say if he will play much again. I hope he does.

The question of eligibility of Irish golfers playing in the Walker Cup team arose in January of 1947, as a result of an article written by American golf critic Lester Rice. And a Reuters' correspondent writing in the *Cork Examiner* added:

> Bruen does now live in Éire (now the Irish Republic) and he entered the British championship from Cork. He was born in Belfast and played in the Walker Cup match in 1938. Presumably, therefore, he is eligible by birth to play on the British team, as is on behalf of the the United States Pasadena-born Bob Sweeney whose home for many years has been England ... Commenting on the doubts thrown on his eligibility by Lester Rice, Mr Bruen told our representative yesterday that he did not see why the question of his eligibility should be raised at this particular time. 'There was no question about it when I played on the British Walker Cup team before,' he said, 'and there was no question about Cecil Ewing who comes from Sligo or John Burke who comes from Lahinch.'

Many Irish golfers would interpret the Lester Rice pronounce-
ment as a considerable compliment to James Bruen since, having
ruled Bruen out of the British team, Rice considered the remainder
of the possible British team as a 'poor crop of amateurs'.

Since then the Royal and Ancient has solved this problem by
calling the Walker Cup team the British and Irish Walker Cup
Team. In that month of January as well, the *Daily Scotsman*, an
Edinburgh newspaper, published a rather nice little poem which
is a great compliment to Jimmy Bruen. It is written by a man who
signs himself 'Signeter' and it reads:

> *Our island is steady and rock-like we know,*
> *Our gallants are ready to slaughter the foe,*
> *And the name that spells ruin to Yank rank and file*
> *Are big Jimmy Bruen and wee Alec Kyle.*
>
> *Though Skee may be Regal and Smiley be quick,*
> *Their occasional eagle will scarce do the trick,*
> *for the names that spell ruin to Yanks on this isle,*
> *Are big Jimmy Bruen and wee Alec Kyle.*

Jimmy did not play in the Walker Cup that year and, as he said
himself, 'It would be unfair of me to try to play unfit, and at the
same time to deprive a fit man who had been practising for his
place in the team'. There is no doubt that Jimmy's wrist that year
was extremely painful and it was on this account that he decided
not to play. There was much regret and Bernard Darwin wrote:
'The loss of Jimmy Bruen was a cruel blow for the British team,
because he was the automatic number one of the side, and it is a
great thing for a team to have a player at the top about whom
there is no doubt'. He also said: 'We shall want all the Irishmen
we can get'.

The acting editor of *Golf Illustrated* wrote at that time in *Irish
Golf*:

> It is bad luck on Bruen sustaining his injury at this time. He would
> most certainly have been spearhead of our Walker Cup team. But
> don't be despondent because you cannot discover another Bruen.
> They are not to be found every day!

Bruen played no golf at all in 1948 but decided that he would
make a comeback in 1949. In that year, Henry Cotton wrote:

Former Amateur champion James Bruen of Cork is back where he left off in 1946 when, by lifting a paving stone, he tore a ligament in his right hand which kept him out of golf for two years. His accident, at first of no moment, developed into a long business to cure and, despite rumours that the powerful Irishman was through with golf, here he is fit again and as large as life ... and still with a burning desire to play golf well again, as he modestly puts it. I had a look at Bruen last week, he came to Royal Mid-Surrey and I made a few – and I hope helpful – suggestions to fix up his game.

I was going to say to take out the kinks. But in Bruen's case I have left the kink there, for the curious 'Bruen Loop' is always going to be there. Over ten years ago I told him not to listen to his critics who said no one can play with that swing.

Last week I once again saw a golf ball travel as I have very rarely seen it in my life. Bruen is colossal and on a cold and windy morning with the hands cold and the grip shiny, not forgetting that the balls were not at their resilient best either, he drove 'a mile'...!

I think that this quite successful insurance broker will yet make golfing history ... Bruen is hoping to play in the Amateur Championship, the Open and the Walker Cup if invited. If we had a few Bruens we could easily win the cup.

At that time, Henry Longhurst wrote too in *The Sunday Times* under the heading 'Big Stuff':

Catching him on one of his fleeting and occasional visits to this country I was able to ask the Royal Mid-Surrey professional for the latest news about Jimmy Bruen whom he has recently been coaching at that club ... In partnership Cotton likes to think they could take on any professional and amateur in the world ... It is Bruen's own impression that he is now hitting the ball further than ever. His wrist has responded to treatment and it is as good as it will ever be and there is no reason why it should ever 'go' again.

Cotton, who has now left for another two-month tour of the Argentina, was moved to extraordinary tributes by Bruen's present form ...

I asked Cotton to what he attributed his length and his answer was 'Just speed of the club head'. Pursued further he could not explain this speed but added this interesting point – that it was to be expected since Bruen could throw a ball further than almost anyone. 'Anyone who can throw a ball can hit one,' he said. He often makes beginners somewhat to their astonishment, throw balls into his net at Monte Carlo.

Apart from recommending adjustment to his grip Cotton made no attempt to change Bruen's style. The celebrated kink remains untouched and the whole business was more a matter of polishing up ...

He seems to have recovered his keenness for the grind of tournament golf – if indeed he ever lost it – and hopes to play not only in the Amateur at Portmarnock but also in the Open at Deal.

For myself I always thought him more likely before the war to win the Open. Anyway his presence will not only add colour to both these tournaments, but will positively 'make' our Walker Cup team. What's more it lends possibilities to a match which the whole of Ireland, and most of England, Scotland and Wales, passport or no passport, will trample upon each other to witness – Bruen versus Stranahan in the final at Portmarnock.

When asked at that time by an *Irish Independent* reporter if he thought his wrist injury would impair him at all, he said: 'While it will never be quite normal, it is as well as ever it will be and hardly affects me at all'.

Yet another golf reporter wrote:

It might take the pen of a Maurice Walsh to wrap romance around an Irish pictorial hero but talk to an Eire golfer, man or woman, about the impressive Jimmy Bruen and you will feel that he is from another world. Wondrous tales reach me of Bruen's amazing powers – far out-stretching that when winning the Amateur title at Birkdale in 1946. I am told that indubitably one of the greatest amateurs … is better than ever. 'He is so strong he forces the ball into the turf with his heel during practice and then smashes it out and sends it to the green with the most remarkable arm force you ever saw,' writes a friend of mine after watching him at play and adds, 'He'll murder Stranahan'.

He never did play Stranahan, so nobody will ever know whether he would have beaten him or not, but I do know that of all the amateurs he had played against and seen playing, he regarded Stranahan as one of the best he had ever seen.

That year there was a one-day trial at Portmarnock on 12 May before the Irish team was selected. The matches were played in three balls, each player playing the other. In the morning Jimmy did not play very well and was beaten by a very much in form Jimmy Carroll of Sutton by 3 and 2, but he beat Cecil Ewing by 1 up in the afternoon. Jimmy played Ray McNally of Sutton and Frank Webster of Skerries and beat McNally by 3 and 2 and Webster by 3 and 2, thus easily ensuring himself a place on the team. I remember that day well as I had the honour also to play in those trials and had a good beating from McNally and 'Brud' Slattery from Lahinch. I played quite well in the afternoon only to be beaten again by Joe Carr 3 and 2 and Billy O'Sullivan 2 and 1.

A week later in Portmarnock, the internationals were played as a pipe-opener to the British Amateur Championship at the same venue the following week. Ireland played Scotland the first day and this was the first time that Jimmy had been partnered with Max McCready (a partnership that was to be very successful for a number of years to come, including the Walker Cup match). This must surely have been Ireland's strongest international team, consisting of James Bruen, Max McCready, Cecil Ewing, J. O'Neill, Joe Carr, Brennie Scannell, John Burke, William O'Sullivan, Jimmy Carroll and Ray McNally, and hopes were high that Ireland would win the triple crown for the first time.

Ireland started in good style, winning all five of the foursomes, and beat Scotland a total of nine matches to three. Quoting from the *Cork Examiner* of the following day:

> As was to be expected, tremendous interest was centred on the reappearance of Jimmy Bruen in both his matches. He was followed by the great majority of the spectators with McCready as his foursome partner. He won the match against Kyle and Dykes with plenty to spare ...
>
> There are rare occasions during championship events when a shot is played of such a spectacular nature that it becomes part of the history of the particular course. Such a shot was played yesterday (Bruen in his singles match against J. B. Stephenson). Bounding the eighteenth fairway at Portmarnock is the roadway and Jimmy's mighty but badly placed drive, shot right across the roadway off the wall of a tent and finished in deep rough at the foot of a sizable hill. Stephenson, dormie 1 at the time, played the drive in the centre of the fairway and proceeded to play what appeared to be a match-winning second onto cut grass beside the green. Bruen knew then he had to get a 3 to save the match, and so impossible did that appear that many spectators walked away confident that the Scot had won. But they reckoned without the Cork player. Getting a line on the hole by climbing the hill he returned to his ball and proceeded to put every ounce into his mashie niblick shot. The perfectly hit ball soared to a great height and, amid astonished silence, it was seen to drop on to the green and finish within 4 feet of the pin. It

was only a matter of form to hole the putt and so was saved the match which appeared to be well and truly lost the minute before.

The following day Ireland faced Wales and beat them by the large margin of 7½ to 2½

Again according to the *Cork Examiner:*

> In the public mind the verdict was practically unanimous that the man to follow was Jimmy Bruen, and both his matches were attended by huge galleries. And what grand golf he played on both outings. Partnered by McCready he found the leading Welsh pair, S. P. McRoberts and J. L. Morgan, strike an inspired spell for the first six holes to give them a lead of three holes. Bruen stopped the rot by sinking a 20-yarder on the seventh for a birdie 2 and upped this by practically driving the 350-yards-long eighth. When his partner pitched in neatly the Cork player holed an 8-foot putt for another win. Turning 1 down the Irish pair squared at the tenth, won the thirteenth, fourteenth and fifteenth. A half at the sixteenth finished the match with Bruen and McCready being one under at this stage. For the six holes from the seventh to the twelfth they required only nineteen shots.

In the afternoon Jimmy Bruen went on to beat the Welsh champion, A. A. Duncan. And so, Ireland and England, both unbeaten, met on the last day, and the winner would win the triple crown. England won the match by seven matches to six and two matches halved, in probably one of the most exciting day's golf ever seen at Portmarnock. I can do nothing better than quote from the *Cork Examiner:*

> It was a sad day for Ireland at Portmarnock yesterday when, by the narrowest of margins, they failed to make golf history by winning the international championship for the first time … It was a day of tremendous excitement for the thousands of spectators and of unforgettable strain for the players on whose individual efforts so much depended for their respective countries.
>
> Amongst those who watched the latter stages of the contest was President O'Kelly who took up an unobtrusive position at the edge of the eighth green and watched several players in succession as they played that hole and drove to the next. Finally, Bruen figured in two matches … In the top foursomes he and McCready faced Ronnie White, the English champion, and almost equally formidable Charlie Stowe. In the early stages the Irishmen looked all set for an easy victory … The Irishmen were out in 35 to the Eng-

lishmen's 37. The lead was reduced to 1 at the eleventh where McCready's drive was off the line and Bruen's second found a bunker. Two halves followed, and then a colossal drive by the Cork player at the fourteenth enabled the Irishmen to get a birdie for 2 up. They slipped up, however, at the short fifteenth when the English pair won in 3. Two long putts by McCready and White halved the sixteenth and, when Bruen pitched to the middle of the seventeenth green and Stowe failed to stay on, all seemed assured. However, White, who had been playing magnificently, chipped to within an inch of the hole and another half resulted. The crowning incident of a truly great match came at the eighteenth when both McCready and White found the green with their seconds, Bruen putted first and the ball stopped within 6 inches of the hole. Stowe studied his putt for quite a time and then proceeded to play off the line of the hole. The Englishman's luck did not desert him, however, as his ball cannoned off the other and into the hole for a 3 which halved the match.

It was an amazing finish to a great match and Stowe had good reason to throw his cap in the air to celebrate his good luck. It turned out that the lucky putt won the Championship for England.

The gallery was so great for Bruen's afternoon match against Gerald Micklem, the Walker Cup player, that every shot from start to finish was played through a line of spectators who barely gave the players room to swing their clubs. In the golfing sense it was not a good match as neither player appeared to be in his best form but every moment of it was exciting.

Micklem won on the seventeenth hole. Jimmy was at times playing his usual brilliant golf. However, there were times when he was not up to his usual standard. Nevertheless, he obviously did more than enough in these internationals to get selected for the Walker Cup team again.

The next weekend all of these great players went to the Royal Dublin Links in Dollymount, near Dublin, to play in the *Golf Illustrated* Gold Vase, played over thirty-six holes. This was won by the English Amateur champion, Ronnie White, with two magnificent rounds of 71 over the 6,600-yard course.

White began his second round three strokes behind twenty-six-year-old Charles Lowrie, youngest member of the Scottish international team, who set up a new amateur record for the course with a brilliant round of 68 (33 and 35) which included three 2s, two strokes behind came Jimmy Bruen, Alec Kyle and Alec Stephenson all on the 70 mark. Lowrie maintained his form to reach the turn in 34 on his second time out, but in the rain and strong wind, which ruined the cards of many, he took 75. Bruen failed on the last few holes, to finish in 148, six shots behind the winner, White. The leading scores in this star-studded field are worth recalling: On 142 R. G. White, Royal Liverpool, 71, 71. On 143 C. D. Lowrie, Honourable Co. of Edinburgh Golfers, 68, 75; J. B. Carr, Sutton, 71, 72. On 146 A. T. Kyle, Sandmore 70, 76. On 147 P.B. Lucas, Sandylodge, 72, 75. On 148 J. M. Dykes, Prestwick, 74, 74; A. D. Lyons, Kilkenny, 71, 77; K. Troy, Royal Dublin, 71, 77; J. Bruen, Cork, 70, 78; W. S. McLeod, Old Renairly, 73, 75; J.B. Bech, Berkshire, 74, 74; A. Stephenson, Prestwick, 70, 78. On 149 C. Evans, USA, 76, 73; L. G. Crawley, Rye, 74, 75; J. Carroll, Sutton, 76, 73; J. C. Browne, Waterford, 71, 78.

The Amateur Championship began the following Monday, 23 May, at Portmarnock, and the first great disappointment came for everybody when James Bruen was scratched from the Championship. The *Cork Examiner* of the following day wrote:

> Two Walker Cup players suffered defeat in the first day's play in the Open Amateur Championship … These were Cecil Ewing, holder of the two Irish titles and Charlie Stowe, the Lancashire man who was runner-up for the English title some weeks ago. The Walker Cup selectors … were given a further shock when it was announced yesterday that Jimmy Bruen, the brilliant twenty-nine-year-old Cork golfer and Amateur champion of 1946, has had to scratch on medical grounds.

I well remember the great disappointment Jimmy's withdrawal from the Championship caused. I happened to be playing in the same championship, and I will never forget the fantastic putting of Tony Duncan whom I met in the first round and who gave me a jolly good beating by 6 and 5, being four under 4s for the whole play. Another interesting memory I have of that Championship is of Redmond Simcox, then not a serious contender for the title. He was at the time a bosom friend of my father's who also happened to enter for this championship, and as luck would have it, the two of them met in the first round. That was undoubtedly one of the most entertaining golf matches in any Championship. These two played golf with each other in the normal way probably once a week, and there they were playing each other in the first round of the Amateur Championship, neither wanting to beat the other not caring which of them won – both retired to the bar after nine holes

Another memory of that Championship which will always remain in my mind is when, in the last eight, Mick Power, another fine Cork golfer, played Willie Turnesa. Having been all square after the eighteenth they went down to the nineteenth where Mick Power had to play an easy No. 9 shot over a bunker and on to the last to get a 4 which Turnesa was never going to get, to beat the great man and probably gain himself a Walker Cup place. But alas, it was not to be. McCready went on to win that championship, beating Turnesa in the final.

I remember also that it was the same Championship in which the Hon. Patrick Campbell defeated William O'Sullivan of Killarney, in about the last eight, which could well have cost William O'Sullivan a Walker Cup place too.

14

WALKER CUP IN AMERICA

In August 1949 Jimmy went to America with the Walker Cup team of that year. This team, captained by Percy Lucas, better known as Laddie Lucas, consisted of Joe Carr, Cecil Ewing, Gerald Micklem, Max McCready, Ernest Milward, Kenneth Thom, Arthur Perowne, Ronnie White and, of course, Jimmy Bruen. It was the first time that a British Walker Cup team had travelled to America in thirteen years, and they arrived off the *Queen Elizabeth* with a very high reputation. The matches were played at the Winged Foot course starting on 19 August. The British team had given themselves plenty of time to acclimatise themselves and had been playing for some length of time with the American-sized ball.

In an article in the *Reporter Despatch* of White Plains, Bill Roche wrote about the Walker Cup:

> The difference in the Winged Foot course and the British course is likely to be an important factor, according to Laddie Lucas. Only three of the eleven men have played on American courses and none has as yet had a turn at the Manaroneck (Winged Foot layout). The matches are slated for the par 72, 6,734-yard championship east course – one of the most difficult in the country and often a scene of many of the top US events. The British trouble will come on the narrow tree-lined, well-bunkered fairways and rolling greens dotted with bottle necks. 'The majority of our courses,' Lucas said yesterday, 'are of the flat type, more broad than narrow with wide entrances'. That is one reason why the British captain is not figuring on accepting too many of the invitations of other eastern courses to practise on their layouts. He'd rather gain a thorough familiarity with the scene of the internationals.

According to an article in the *Cork Examiner* on the day before the match, written by Pat Heffernan, Reuters' special New York correspondent:

> The four Irish members of the British team were included in the foursomes, with Bruen and McCready partners for the second

match. At practice Joe Carr, another of the Irishmen, and Ronnie White have shown themselves to be an ideal pairing. Cecil Ewing, the fourth Irishman, and Gerald Micklem have the task of meeting the only American pairing who had also played in the 1947 match, Ted Bishop and Skee Regal, who on that occasion beat Carr and Ewing ... One of the main surprises in the American team is the partnership of Frank Stranahan and Willie Turnesa ... Those dropped from the American team were J. T. McHale and C. R. Coe.

The British Walker Cup golfers sprang two surprises yesterday when they presented their pairings for the foursomes. First Lucas, the left-handed captain of the invading forces, scratched himself in favour of the nineteen-year-old Arthur Perowne, a newcomer to big time golf, because, Lucas said, he was off his game. Second, Lucas dropped what many experts consider the strongest pair, McCready and Bruen, two husky Irishmen, into the number two position on the team.

The result is that in the opening match Turnesa and Billows ... will meet Carr and White. Bruen and McCready will face the number two American combination of Stranahan and Kocsis ... Third duo will match Regal and Bishop, both former American Amateur champions, against Ewing and Micklem ... Going off last is the youngster Perowne and his almost equally young partner, Thom, who will face the two oldest players on the American team, Dawson and McCormick, both over forty ... The measure of interest in the British side is greater than usual, so too is the confidence placed in their efforts to arrest the trophy which the Americans so decisively gained at St Andrew's in 1947. The team itself settled down for steady team practice under the leadership of P. B. Lucas, the results of which were evident when the amateurs met a professional side at Royal Mid-Surrey before they left for America. The meeting was, of course, only a try-out and the victory as expected went to the professionals but in each game the Walker Cup team showed such magnificent form as to establish great expectations in their meeting with the Americans. The most gratifying outcome of that match was the return to form of James Bruen ... After this period of training in England the British team sailed for America and for the past fortnight have been practising on the Winged Foot course where the Cup match will be played ... the latest reports from New York are that Bruen is in his most majestic form though not yet quite happy about the greens. New York sportswriters have devoted much of their space to the invading British golfing team at Manaroneck with emphasis on the Irishmen. George Trevor in the *New York Sun* wrote: '... The Winged Foot Club, which has a large Irish-American membership is delighted with the complexion of

the British team and foresees fat gate receipts because of that factor....' On the other hand, that shrewd golf writer, Lester Rice, in
the *Journal American* said the American team is highly in favour to
win the Walker Cup.

The match started the next day and it seemed that Rice's predic-
tion was correct. Arthur McWeeney, the well-known golf writer
in the *Irish Independent* was at Winged Foot and reported:

Great Britain and Ireland made a disappointing start to the Walker
Cup match and the final score of the foursomes was the United
States three matches, Great Britain and Ireland one. Thus, with eight
singles remaining to be played, the visitors would appear to have
but a slim chance of recording their second success in the series. For
the perspiring sportswriters it was a case of tear it up and start again,
for the two top matches proved a tremendous tussle in which it
was impossible to anticipate the final result. Joe Carr and Ronnie
White had to pass through a very anxious period in the second half
in their encounter with Willie Turnesa and Ray Billows after looking at one time as if they were set for an easy victory, while Jimmy
Bruen and Max McCready made a wonderful recovery after being
3 down with nine to play against Frank Stranahan and Charles
Kocsis. They squared the match at the fifteenth but could not maintain their efforts and lost eventually by 2 and 1. It turned out rather
in the way we had secretly feared it would. The cool, efficient
Americans excelled us in the short game and on the greens and our
White-Carr combination alone had the ability to match them in
these phases of the game. The weather conditions cannot be offered
as an alibi for their comparatively poor showing by the visiting
team for there was a strong breeze during the morning and, while
it dropped somewhat in the afternoon, the temperature was never
unduly high. Carr and White played magnificent golf ... The all-
English combination of Ken Thom and nineteen-year-old Arthur
Perowne just had not sufficient metal for the job ... But ... the big
story of the day was the battle which McCready and Bruen put up
in the afternoon and the last seven holes in the match were certainly dramatic stuff ... McCready and Bruen deserve the greatest credit for their magnificent fight – theirs was the match which captured
the biggest gallery of the day and held it too until the final stroke –
but they could never quite match the feather-like touch which
Stranahan displayed in playing some bunkers, or equally the heart-
breaking putting of the solidly passive Kocsis.

I have mentioned that Carr and White had to survive an anxious period during their progress to victory by 3 and 2. This is

when the Americans whittled back two of the three holes which our pair had started the afternoon round with.

Turnesa and Billows, whose driving had been shaky throughout the match, were at this stage putting very well – Turnesa having found the hole with a 5-yarder at the twenty-eighth and a 3-yarder at the twenty-seventh. At this juncture White showed his mettle by playing a superb recovery shot when Carr underclubbed himself at the twenty-eighth to snatch a half. Then they played the twenty-ninth steadily to halve it in 4 and they won the thirtieth – Billows played a poor approach. The moment of crisis was over and the Anglo-Irish partnership was firmly set on the path to victory. For the singles the following day Lucas made no change in his team, which was somewhat surprising as it was felt he should have played Milward and, indeed, himself.

It is, of course, history that America won the match by ten matches to two, winning all bar one of the singles. Ronnie White was the only winner for the British side, beating Willie Turnesa.

Man for man the British amateurs seemed to be able to drive longer and there was not much to choose in their long iron shots. Within 150 feet of the green, however, the Americans were sounder. The difficult short holes also cost the British much ground. Time and again they were trapped in bunkers and needed 2 to reach the green. That put the pressure on them so far as putting was concerned, and they usually failed to withstand it. Bruen started the match with Regal by winning the first hole with a superb 3, but then he had to bow before a storm of better than par figures. Regal being three under 4s for the next six holes, four of which he won. It looked like being a rout when Bruen failed to find the green at the tenth to lose to a 3 and then he dropped the 300-yard eleventh to another 3. However, he came right back with a great counterattack, winning the thirteenth, fourteenth and fifteenth in 3, 4, 4.

He was back in 35 having a round of 72 which left him two holes in arrears. Bruen lost two more holes in the outward half in the afternoon and he was 4 down after twenty-seven holes, Regal eventually winning by 5 and 4.

Joe Carr also had a bad day from Johnny Dawson and never recovered from it.

Of the Irishmen, Cecil Ewing, the oldest player on the side, probably played the best golf and certainly made a gallant effort against Charlie Coe. He eventually found himself dormie 3 down to Coe, the youngest American. He then shot an eagle 3 at the sixteenth and a birdie 4 at the seventeenth to keep the match alive. He had a curly 12-foot putt to halve the match at the eighteenth, he hit it well but it just curled away from the hole at the last minute and Coe got a half in 4 and he was able to win the match by one hole.

In all, this British side, which looked very strong on paper, in fact got a very bad beating, but they were up against what many people considered to be one of the strongest American teams to line out in the Walker Cup, and their captain, Laddie Lucas, expressed the sentiments of the team when he said: 'We have no regrets and no excuses, we were beaten by a great American side'.

During that American trip the British team paid a visit to the Pine Valley course and, as far as I know, Jimmy only played that course once. In his scrapbook there is a card of a round that he played there which reads:

> At the first hole, par 4, Bruen 3. At the second hole, par 4, Bruen 4. Third hole, par 3, Bruen 3. Fourth hole, par 4, Bruen 4. Fifth hole, par 3, Bruen 3. Sixth hole, par 4, Bruen 6. Seventh hole, par 4, Bruen 5. Eighth hole, par 4, Bruen 4. Ninth hole, par 4, Bruen 5. Par 34, Bruen 37. Tenth hole, par 3, Bruen 3. Eleventh hole, par 4, Bruen 4. Twelfth hole, par 4, Bruen 4. Thirteenth hole, par 4, Bruen 4. Fourteenth hole, par 3, Bruen 3. Fifteenth hole, par 5, Bruen 5. Sixteenth hole, par 4, Bruen 4. Seventeenth hole, par 4, Bruen 5. Eighteenth hole, par 4, Bruen 4.

For the second nine, a 35 par, Bruen took 36, giving him a total of 73 – obviously a good round on this extremely difficult course.

After the Walker Cup, the British team went to Rochester in New York to play in the US Amateur Golf Championship. This was played at the Oak Hill golf course in early September. The weather conditions were very bad, and some of the matches in the first round had to be stopped. This apparently had never happened in this championship previously. Unfortunately, Jimmy was beaten in the first round by twenty-one-year-old George Bigham of Kansas city.

On returning from America, Jimmy went into virtual retirement from big golf and did not emerge again until the internationals in September of the following year, 1950.

On the first day, Ireland played Scotland and, once again with Max McCready, Jimmy played in the top foursome. They beat A. T. Kyle and J. B. Stephenson by 3 and 2. They got off to a flying start and at the very first hole McCready holed from 15 yards to give his side a win with a 3. When he hit the pin with his chip at the 149-yard seventh, he and his partner stood 4 up. Kyle and Stephenson never looked like stopping the rot and only managed to win one hole, the fourteenth, before the Irishmen won the match with a half at the fifteenth. Although McCready and Bruen, particularly the latter, had not played much golf that season their partnership was perhaps the most powerful of the day. Nevertheless, Scotland defeated Ireland by three matches to two in the foursomes and, owing to a huge downpour of rain which flooded the course on that Wednesday, the singles had to be postponed to the following Saturday.

Against Wales the next day, when Ireland won by seven matches to three, again the Bruen and McCready combination won the top foursomes and – along with wins by Cecil Ewing and Cecil Beamish and Joe Carr with Brendan Herlihy – gave Ireland a lead of three to two. Bruen and McCready beat M. A. Jones and W. J. Roberts by 4 and 3 being level 4s for fifteen holes over this course of Royal St David, Harlech. The Irishmen had the extra length from the tee which was a telling factor in the bad weather. They won the sixth, seventh and eighth holes to be 3 up and, although they lost the short ninth where McCready pushed his tee shot, the pair made amends at the next hole, eventually finishing the match on the fifteenth.

In the singles, Jimmy played A. A. Duncan in one of the best matches of that day. Bruen played great golf, as his score of 68 showed. This comprised two halves of 34 each. Yet he was unable to shake off the Welshman. At the turn Bruen was 1 up. He increased this to 2 at the tenth but Duncan, with a 2 at the eleventh and an eagle 3 at the twelfth, squared and although each went one hole up over the next few holes they were again square with three to play, and they gallantly finished, halving the last three holes.

On the Friday Ireland played England and after a fine performance they had a lead of 4 and 1 in the foursomes. Again McCready and Bruen led the Irish team and beat P. F. Scrutton and

R. Tredinnick by 3 and 2. The Englishmen matched their opponents shot for shot most of the way but McCready and Bruen stood 1 up at the eleventh. They kept ahead winning the fourteenth and fifteenth, and finished in two under 4s for the sixteen holes played. In the afternoon Jimmy played S. Tredinnick and he was beaten 2 and 1. This came as a bit of a shock to the Irish supporters for Bruen was not as reliable as usual on the greens, and against a consistent golfer he found himself 3 down at the ninth. Tredinnick gave an instance of his ability at the tenth. He lost his ball from the tee but nevertheless got a 3 with his second ball, holing a 10-yard putt to be 4 up. Bruen, however, fought bravely and reduced his deficit to two holes by winning the thirteenth and fourteenth, but Tredinnick was not to be shaken. He halved the next three holes to make certain of victory.

So, with England and Wales beaten, Ireland went out on the Saturday morning to play the postponed singles against Scotland. In this match Jimmy played well-known Scottish golfer W. S. McLeod. Bruen was 1 down at the turn which he reached in 36. He levelled at the tenth but had a grim struggle the rest of the way. He stood 1 up after sixteen holes, halved the seventeenth and had a piece of bad luck on the home green. He was laid a dead stymie only 8 inches from the hole and failed in an attempt to lift the ball into the Tin, while McLeod holed his putt to halve the match. Thus, Ireland halved with Scotland and won the Championship for the first time. However, there was some disappointment that they had not beaten Scotland which would have given them the elusive triple crown.

In November of that year Jimmy played in the *Daily Telegraph* Amateur Professional Foursomes at Formby and there is an excellent description by the late A. P. McWeeney in *Irish Golf*:

> The *Daily Telegraph* Amateur Professional Tournament is something very special in the golfing calendar. It is a most attractive competition from the spectators' point of view and it is staged in the grand manner with every possible comfort and facility provided for the competitors and the press ...
>
> Entry into the *Daily Telegraph* competition is by invitation as far as the amateurs are concerned, while the professionals to the tune of thirty-two secure their places through the PGA Averages for the season's tournaments. Ireland was honoured by eight players in the event, six amateurs and two professionals, the latter being Fred

Daly and Harry Bradshaw and the former J. Bruen, M. McCready, C. A. Beamish, J. J. Carroll, J. Glover and N. Drew.

This was a useful team enough but the standard of the competition was so hot that we were hopeful more than confident that an Irishman would win for the first time. And an Irishman did succeed in the person of James Bruen who, in partnership with Londoner Wally Smithers, battled his way through five rounds to record a splendid victory. This foursome game has a particular fascination in the fact that two of the best individual players in an event such as this do not necessarily make the best combination ...

This ability to combine was one of the main reasons for the success of Bruen and Smithers. From the very start this partnership slipped smoothly into top gear with each man doing his share in cool competent fashion, and with neither ever becoming ruffled when the other made a mistake. Smithers, a cheerful workman-like golfer, quite plainly enjoyed playing with a long-hitting partner, and he can send the ball quite a distance himself and it is his temperament to adopt a bold policy. He and Bruen were always attacking in their matches and that is one of the principal reasons why they came through. A contributing factor too was Bruen's cool consideration in chipping and putting. Time after time he left the ball beside the hole from off the green, and when he rolled up a long putt it almost always finished adjacent to the pin ...

The first round saw the elimination of young Norman Drew. He and John Burton finding the favourites R. White and R. Burton a shade too good for them and the all-Irish combination of J. P. Carroll and H. Bradshaw also fell at this stage. They never struck their best form against G. P. Roberts and Fred Daly.

The issue was really joined on the second day and when the smoke of battle had died down one discovered that the only Irishman left in was James Bruen. C. H. Beamish and his Ryder Cup partner, K. Bousfield, had cracked badly against Ronnie White and Dick Burton while Bruen and Smithers had put paid to the account of Fred Daly and his partner. M. McCready, who was partnered by the Scotsman, Laurie Ayton, came a bad cropper for he cracked in the most unexpected fashion in the closing stages of their match with M. Jones and W. J. Branch, and they lost when they failed with a 4-foot putt at the nineteenth. John Glover, the Boys' champion, who was paired with the lanky R. A. Knight, played quite well and it was not until the quarter final that they found opposition too strong for them in the person of John Langley, English native champion and Sid Scott. Glover showed that he was the right temperament for big golf, and his short game was most favourably commented upon by the experts. *[The author clearly has made an error here in not including John Glover amongst the Irish players.]*

In the meantime, Bruen and Smithers were fighting desperately against J. W. Jones, the English international, and Johnny Fallon, the Huddersfield professional. 1 down and four to play they rose to the occasion in a magnificent fashion to finish 3, 3, 3, 4 and won on the last green ...

As for the final, the golf correspondent in *The Times* described it as follows:

> The lasting memory of the golf played by the winners will not be the strangely contrasted unorthodoxy of their styles nor the terrible power of Bruen's immense driving and iron play but some of the finest approaching and putting that can ever have been seen in a foursome tournament. Bruen and Smithers were a perfect blend and in every round were absolutely complimentary to each other. Except on the rarest occasion, a mistake by either of them was promptly remedied by the other. He who partners himself with Bruen must be prepared to find himself in strange places and when one of Bruen's projectile-like strokes went soaring into the rough or sandhills Smithers with almost joyful determination would tackle and invariably succeed in the task of recovery. Conversely, when Smithers missed the green, the impressive Irishman played one of his exquisitely judged chips or run-up shots. One lost count of the number of times they needed but one putt. Both putted superbly from any distance; Bruen on the greens is a true artist with the touch of a surgeon.

Another fascinating description of this final was written by Henry Longhurst in *The Sunday Times*:

> It was a typical Formby day with a nip in the air and the wind whistling through the fir trees that divide the course from the seashore – very much a day for strong man's golf.
>
> Branch and Jones worked wonders to reach the final and their appearance therein was a great credit to both. Branch has for many years been in the top flight but has lacked the stamina to last through an Open Championship on the modern 7,000-yards courses ... His partner comes from the Maesdu Club (which I understand to be pronounced 'mizedee') and his talents have long been recognised in Wales ...
>
> Of the winners I can only say how refreshing it was to watch them play. Smithers, like one of the golfing characters of P. G. Wodehouse, 'never spares himself to do the ball a violent injury'. He hits

at it as hard as he possibly can and doesn't mind who knows it.

Bruen of course has the distinction of employing a style quite different from that of any other first-class player either now or, so far as I know, in the game's history. If the man who was standing beside me at Rochester, New York during the last year's United States Championship and remarked 'That guy's swing drives me crazy', had been here today, he would by now have been in the asylum.

At the top of the swing Bruen's club is pointing as near as may be over the top of his head towards the tee box. From here he whips it down with a vicious strength which more than once has broken the handle in his hands, hitting the ball sometimes a distance which is hard to credit unless you have actually seen it.

One or two of his drives today touched the 350 yards and, playing a down wind iron to the eleventh, his ball had such a stop on it as to jerk backwards after its third bounce.

The final, despite the margin, was by no means a one-sided affair. The winners soon went to 3 up, and out in 37 and 2 up. Then Bruen missed a putt and it was anybody's game. Smithers rammed one cheerfully in from 6 feet at the twelfth and they were still 2 up with four to play when the proceedings were enlivened by a rabbit darting the whole way around the green unable to find a way out through the packed gallery. Bruen's second was a high hook. Jones almost holed from 12 yards – how the ball stayed out I could not fathom – whereupon Bruen holed out from 6 yards. Striding to the sixteenth tee he laid his ball a yard from the hole for a 2 and that was that.

Another correspondent described the same match:

Bruen has been the talking point of world golf for a dozen years. Only in the past fortnight in the international series has he come into the limelight over major rivalry in these islands since he won the Amateur Championship four years ago … After his championship success in 1946 his arm trouble developed and was the subject of rumour and report that he might never play in big events again. There was certainly no sign of physical handicap at Formby.

Bruen still has the almost fantastic loop at the top of his swing, and he appears to have lost nothing of his tremendous power, and his short game merged efficiently with that of Smithers in all their matches. They also covered well for each other when necessary with strong recovery play. When Smithers, who is forty-four and a 'have-a-go type of golfer', was warned that he might have to face a recovery problem, his cheerful reply was, 'You hit them where you

like Jimmy and I'll play them'. This remark of Smithers must surely have summed up the approach of these two golfers to the tournament

15

1951 Walker Cup

As a result of his excellent win with Wally Smithers, Jimmy was again in the trials for the Walker Cup team in 1951. These were played at Birkdale on 5, 6, and 7 April, roughly a month before the match itself. At the end of the trials Jimmy, along with Joe Carr, Cecil Ewing and Max McCready, were on the Walker Cup team – a great triumph for Ireland. Four of the ten men on the team were Irish.

Clearly, Jimmy Bruen was still a great golfer but the practice matches proved that he was not 100 per cent 'match fit' and there can be little doubt that his damaged wrist was affecting his play. A month later the team arrived in Birkdale and the day before the match the *Cork Examiner* golfing correspondent wrote:

> The odds are in favour of the United States who have beaten Britain on every occasion except one since the inception of the competition in 1922. However, all the British players are playing very well and it is not impossible that they should win, despite a very strong team from across the Atlantic.
>
> The event starts with the foursomes played over the thirty-six holes and the following are the pairings: R. J. White, Royal Liverpool and J. B. Carr, Sutton *v.* F. Stranahan, Ohio and W. Campbell, West Virginia. In the second match Cecil Ewing, Co. Sligo and J. D. A. Langley, Stoke Poges *v.* C. Coe, Oklahoma and J. McHale, Pennsylvania. A. Kyle, Sandmore and I. Caldwell, Walton Heath *v.* R. Chapman, North Carolina and R. Knowles, South Carolina. In the fourth match J. Bruen, Cork and J. L. L. Morgan, Llandridnod Wells *v.* W. Turnesa, New York and S. Urzetta, New York.

For Jimmy Bruen, the first day of the Walker Cup match was to be a tragic one, in the course of which his wrist completely collapsed. The *Cork Examiner* reported:

> Britain's hopes of a golfing success over the United States in the Walker Cup match in Birkdale, Lancs, have practically disappeared at the end of the first day of a hectic battle when the Americans won the 36-hole foursomes by two matches to nil with two halved. The result was a bitter disappointment to the thousands of specta-

tors who swarmed over the sunbathed course cheering friend and foe alike, in what must have been one of the greatest foursome tussles in the thirty-years history of these encounters. Three of the four matches finished on the home green and were in doubt to the end.

It was a bitter blow when in the middle of his first round match Jimmy Bruen's right wrist gave out. The great-hearted Irishman played on bravely, though being in agonies of pain every time he hit a shot. The wrist had swollen to double its normal size by the time he and Morgan reached the eighteenth green. Despite heroic efforts by the Welshman they could not hope to survive against such a formidable combination as Willie Turnesa the American captain and the reigning US champion, Sam Urzetta.

Ronald Murman, writing in the *Daily Mail* about the same day's golf, said:

The Americans have done it again. In the first day of the Walker Cup match once more they came from 'behind' and tonight 6,000 self-appointed British coroners – the home fans who watched – are delivering their verdict – 'failure due to lack of stamina'.

Four foursome games ended with two victories for America and two games halved … the Americans went out in the afternoon and wedged and putted their way through, poker-faced and unrelenting, to a position which lengthened the odds against the British winning the Walker Cup match at least to 10 to 1. One alibi for Britain's failure … was the fact that James Bruen was a passenger in the afternoon.

… when he went out after lunch his right hand was already a swollen purple thing – 'It feels like a balloon and is terribly painful even on the shortest putt,' he told me.

This was one match Britain had to write off …

Our top player, local boy, Ronnie White, and lanky Irishman Joe Carr were held to an all-square result when big Bill Campbell from Virginia slotted a most awkward putt.

Cecil Ewing and John Langley needed only a half at the end to win but Langley's second shot landed in a terrible position and was unplayable.

Jimmy, of course, did not play the following day in the singles and once again the Walker Cup went back to America.

It was a tragic end to Jimmy Bruen's Walker Cup career. After this match Jimmy played no golf at all for the rest of 1951 and virtually all of 1952. In 1953 the Internationals were scheduled to be held in June in Killarney, which as far as Cork golfers were concerned was just on their doorstep, being a mere 50 miles away. Many young players including myself were striving to get onto that Irish team. Easter fell in the month of April and, as usual, the Cork Scratch Cup was played on our home course. That year that competition had been ear-marked as a trial for the Irish team. In the qualifying round on a blustery day off the back tees Jimmy Bruen easily led the field with a 70 and, though somewhat lucky to survive some of the subsequent rounds, he fought his way to the final. Of the four matches he played, two had gone the full distance and another had gone to three tie holes. I had beaten W. M. O'Sullivan in the quarter-final and Larry McCarthy in the semi-final and found myself in the final against Jimmy. While this match was just another one for Jimmy it was for me one that I shall never forget. I quote from *The Irish Times:*

> G. F. Crosbie, a scratch player from the home club, defeated James Bruen, the Walker Cup player, by two and one in the final of the Cork Scratch Cup. The standard of golf produced by both players was remarkably high and it was accounted the best final ever in the event. Bruen, having gained a lead of one hole in the morning, had 71 and Crosbie 72 and for the thirty-five holes played Crosbie was three under 4s and Bruen only two strokes worse.
>
> Bruen got off to an excellent start being 2 up after six holes but Crosbie took the eighth and ninth to square. Crosbie led for the first time at the eleventh, became 2 up at the thirteenth and then Bruen won the last three holes of the round to gain an interval lead of one hole.
>
> The first five holes in the afternoon were halved but a birdie 3 enabled Crosbie to square at the twenty-fourth. At the next, a short one, Crosbie holed a long putt for 2 while Bruen failed to make the green, but the Walker Cup man squared again at the twenty-sixth while Crosbie took 3 to reach the green. They halved the next five in par and at the thirty-third Bruen put his tee shot out of bounds and Crosbie became 1 up with four to go. Bruen just managed to halve the thirty-third by getting down in a chip and a putt. Crosbie became dormie at the thirty-fourth with a birdie 3 and a half at the next gave him a 2 and 1 win.

Jimmy, who always took an interest in my golf, said, 'Now surely you will get your Irish cap'. He seemed to be as pleased with my win as if he had won himself. That was the Jimmy Bruen I knew. Of course he was right. I did get my place on the Irish team for it was regarded as some achievement to beat Jimmy Bruen, even in those days, over thirty-six holes. In fact, I think it was the only occasion in championship conditions that Jimmy was ever beaten in a 36-hole final.

Later on in that month of April we in Cork Golf Club, through the influence of James Bruen, had the great attraction of watching two exhibition matches in which Henry Cotton was our notable visitor. On the Friday I had the privilege of playing with Henry Cotton against James Bruen and Tom Egan, and it seemed that without the slightest effort Henry Cotton equalled the professional record for the course with a beautifully played 66. I can well remember that had he not taken a 3 to get down from the back of the seventeenth green where he took a 5, Cotton would have broken the record. He and I easily defeated Jimmy and Tom Egan on that day, when neither was at his best.

The following day Henry Cotton teamed up with W. M. O'Sullivan against Jimmy and John McKenna, a local professional from Douglas, for the second match. Tony Goodridge described the match in *The Irish Times*:

> The huge gallery that set out in the wake of the exhibition match at Cork on Saturday in which Henry Cotton and W. M. O'Sullivan beat James Bruen and John McKenna … had an excellent return for their money, for the golf of all four was worthy of the occasion. Over the first nine holes it was McKenna who had the edge on the others. At that point he was two under 4s due in particular to an excellent pitch at the third and a great putt at the ninth which brought him a birdie in each case. O'Sullivan cracked the ball so far from the tee that one sometimes forgot that he still had to play his second shot. He was out in 35 and Bruen and Cotton were both out in 36
>
> Coming home the story was very different and it was Cotton and Bruen who held the stage and the former produced another of these excellent and effortless runs which brought him back in 31 for a gross of 67. In fact from the seventh hole onwards he was eight under 4s. Bruen too played golf which gave him great satisfaction. He was home in 34 which might well have been less, for fate could have treated him a little better on the greens. Three times on the way home his ball just glided over the top of the hole without dropping. He was putting well and all round was playing good, sound, attacking golf. O'Sullivan did not quite sustain on the way home

the high level that he had set himself on the journey out but he had little to worry him for his partner after all was back in 31 and that does not leave much room for other individual talent to intrude itself. McKenna did all and indeed more than was asked of him. With his leisurely effortless swing he is always a pleasure to watch and ... both he and his partner Bruen finished in 70.

Henry Cotton's rounds of 66 and 67 were both immaculate.

Jimmy declined to play in the internationals that year and in fact played no more top golf. However, in the autumn of that year, he did have one achievement worth recording. The *Cork Examiner* reported:

> James Bruen playing off plus 1 came right back to the top of his form yesterday with an amazing 66 gross, 6 under par to win the President's Prize at Cork Golf Club. This great score gave him 41 points in the stableford competition, a total of which was two points better than his nearest rivals ... Playing impressive golf the former Walker Cup player was the model of consistency ...: Out – 4, 5, 4, 4, 4, 3, 3, 4, 3 = 34. Home – 3, 4, 4, 3, 3, 4, 4, 3, 4 = 32. In the afternoon four-ball ... Bruen gave another terrific performance when, in partnership with R. D. Lord, he returned a 64 gross. This score put the partners 11 up on par and far ahead of the rest of the field to enable them to romp home easy winners.

How many people would give their eyes just to have one day's golf like that?

One summer in the 1950s, Jimmy and I happened to be in Ballybunion with our families when we played a little 'holiday' golf together. Ballybunion is a wonderful seaside links on the coast of Kerry. On this same course Jimmy had won his first Irish Close Championship and anyone who has played it will know that it ranks among the very top links courses in Great Britain and Ireland. There happened on this July Sunday to be a 'one club' competition on in the club so Jimmy and I, armed with a No. 5 iron each, entered. That day I was witness to an extraordinary round of golf. Off not the very back tees, but the competition tees, he holed this great course in 72 with only his No. 5 iron. It was an incredible performance. I saw a variety of shots that day that I am unlikely to see again. I can't remember what handicap he was playing off – it must have been about +2 or +3 but I know his net score of 74 or 75 won the competition by at least ten strokes – there was nobody within a mile of him.

16

BRUEN V. CARR

From 1953 to 1960 Jimmy Bruen played virtually no serious golf. He did, however, turn out most years in the Castletroy Scratch Cup in Limerick which is a 36-hole competition, and he won that in the process. The next newspaper account we read of him is just prior to his election in 1960 as an Irish selector. In December 1959 Sam McKinlay, an old friend of his, wrote in the *Glasgow Herald:*

> James Bruen has been appointed a member of the Irish International Selection Committee and will thus once again exert influence on a game which he adorned for a year or two before the war and, until his wrist gave out, again after the war. It is not to be supposed that selector Bruen will help to produce golfers of his own remarkable calibre. He was *sui generis* possibly the only golfing genius these islands have produced since Vardon ...
>
> At his best he hit the ball further than anyone else, professional or amateur. He was also, especially before the war, one of the best putters in the game, bold almost to a fault and wonderfully deft and accurate. He could extract the ball from impossible places and not only get it back into play but as often as not put it within holing distance. There has never been a golfer who could hit the ball from sand as far and as accurate as Bruen. He was in short the complete golfer and goodness knows what he might have done if the war had not cut his career in half.
>
> His record is not so good as that of his great fellow countryman, Joe Carr, partly because he did not have Carr's tremendous competitive compulsion. But when Bruen's imagination was alight and when his 'loop' was working and when he was not breaking steel shafts like matchsticks he was the most thrilling accomplished golfer in the world. His presence and prematch performance made our solitary Walker Cup victory possible. Perhaps his new position will stimulate Irish golf to some of the heights he reached and in the process British golf will benefit.

About the same time 'Metro' in the *Cork Examiner* wrote:

> There will be tremendous welcome in golfing circles all over Ireland at the choice of three great players, James Bruen, Dr W. M.

O'Sullivan and Cecil Ewing as selectors for next season – and possibly for many seasons to come. This is a really progressive step for, while giving full credit to our recent body of selectors, there are obvious advantages of having men on the job who have been through the severe mental and physical ordeal of the international occasion both at Walker Cup and home international level.

What a splendid thing it is to see Bruen ready to take an active part in the game again. I have always maintained that Bruen ranked second only to Bobby Jones … I will not budge an inch from my claim … even with Joe Carr supporters prepared to assail me.

Bruen is not yet forty, yet to the younger generation he is no more than a legend, for his last appearance in an international championship was in 1946 when he won the British title in Birkdale … he never competed in an Irish championship after the war and so he remains a shadowy if mighty figure to those who have come to the fore in the last seven or eight years.

That he will be a sound judge of young talent seems certain for he was a keen student in every aspect of the game in his playing days. How strange and sad it is to reflect that, but for the injury to his wrist which developed so soon after his triumph at Birkdale and got progressively worse, he might still have been one of the best players in the world.

That year too Jimmy turned out in the British Amateur Championship which was played in Royal Portrush. His appearance was a very short one and is described well by Frank Pennink:

> For a long time we saw golf's most famous 'loop' in action again when the Amateur Championships began in rain-swept Portrush yesterday. Jimmy Bruen … decided to chance the suspect wrist which kept him out of competitive golf for so long. But with the notorious short hole, the fourteenth, aptly named 'Calamity Corner' to come and his wrist badly swollen, he chose wisely to concede the match, though 4 up, to Billy Steele, the recent Oxford Blue. 'This is the finish of my championship golf,' said Bruen. Perhaps now he looked more like lassoing one steer rather than a whole herd but his famous whip-like swing had stirred old memories … and his premature withdrawal … into the new role as an Irish selector is much to be deplored.

Over these years there were to be many discussions at the nineteenth hole of many a golf club as to whether Joe Carr or James Bruen was the better player. Like all such arguments there is, of course, no definitive conclusion. Two things, however, are certain: firstly, they were undoubtedly the two best amateurs that we have produced in this country; and secondly, although they met on two occasions the results cannot be said to prove anything, for certainly Bruen was not at his peak when these matches were played. However, as these two players are so often compared, a description of these matches is, I think, of great interest.

For many years Cork Golf Club played Sutton Golf Club annually, and in 1963 we persuaded Jimmy to play. There is a description of this match in the *Cork Examiner* of the following day:

> Joe Carr had to go all the way at Cork Golf Club yesterday to defeat James Bruen in one of the most talked about golf matches played in the south for many years … However, the victory was of no benefit to Sutton and they were well beaten by Cork in this inter-club challenge, the final margin being a surprising 7 to 2….
>
> In the clash between Carr and Bruen, only the second time they have met … people were surging around the last green to watch as Bruen narrowly failed with a 10-yard putt to save the match. Carr was ahead all the time from the seventh being 3 to the good at the turn, but he had to withstand a storming recovery by Bruen which clearly indicated that the man who is now a selector is still very much a force as a player. In addition it was only the Corkman's fourth game since last August. The figures, despite a 6 each on the first nine, were good. Carr being two under par 73 for the eighteen. Bruen started very well, leaving a long putt dead for a winning 4 at the first and Carr put his second into the sand. But watched by an eager following the Corkman knocked his second tee shot into the bushes and then put his next attempt into the field on the right and out of bounds. A slack approach to the fourth green cost Bruen a 6 and Carr led by getting his regulation 5, but the situation was reversed at the next, this time Carr being short with his chip and losing with a 6 to 5. They halved the sixth but then came the turning point….
>
> Bruen was short at the 3-par seventh and then missed a 2-foot putt to lose the hole and go 1 down. At the eighth Carr, after watching Bruen leave a great shot 2 inches from the pin, holed out a 40-yarder 8 iron for a winning eagle 2. Obviously shaken by this, Bruen temporarily lost his golden putting touch at the ninth and took 3 putts to lose again and turned 3 down to Carr.
>
> But then started the recovery which kept the rapidly growing gallery scurrying frantically for vantage points.
>
> Bruen took a safe 4 at the tenth and Carr mis-hit his putt to lose

the hole. A chip from the left of the green at the eleventh followed by a wicked 7-foot putt brought Bruen a winning birdie and cut the arrears to a single hole. Carr hit the longest drive of the day at the twelfth but a masterly approach gave Bruen a half in 4.

Both men found the short thirteenth and here Bruen, putting second, left a 9-foot putt a few inches short of the cup and had to settle for a half. When he went through the fourteenth green, his ball landing on the drier part of the putting surface, the pressure was really on but he came back by halving the hole in 4.

However, he could not get a half at the fifteenth, missing a 6-foot putt. 2 down he brought a roar of encouragement from the gallery when he slammed a huge drive down the sixteenth fairway, put his second iron on the green and dropped a 10-yarder for a winning birdie. Carr played it safe off the tricky seventeenth tee using a 2 iron, but even so he was fortunate to get the half in 4. Bruen found himself lying awkwardly on the grassy edge of a sand bunker on the left. So awkwardly was it in fact that twice he fell off balance as he attempted to address the ball. Eventually he held the shaft in the centre and, playing a masterly stroke, almost holed out. The eighteenth saw Carr leave his first putt dead and forced Bruen to hole out from about 12 yards to save the match. He narrowly failed and victory was Carr's.

In the morning Bruen had been in even better form playing with George Crosbie and blitzing Carr and Mick Fitzpatrick to the tune of 5 and 4. He played some exceptionally long shots, including one beauty at the eleventh and was putting magnificently. Crosbie too was in his best form here and between them they gave the visitors no chance at all. They were level fours when the match finished.

I remember one rather interesting and amusing incident which occurred in the foursomes that morning. We were playing the eleventh hole which is a very long par 4 of 460 odd yards, against the wind. Both Michael Fitzpatrick and I hit rather indifferent drives, but mine was on the fairway. Jimmy took out his driver and hit one of the most colossal shots I have ever seen straight into the middle of that green from a position none of us thought was possible. Joe Carr was so intrigued with this shot that he decided to drop a ball at the same place to see if he could emulate it. This, of course, was possible as this was but a friendly inter-club match. However, although he tried two or three times, Joe didn't get within 20 yards of the green, and he admitted afterwards that it was a fantastic shot.

In June of that year the Irish Close Championship was played in Killarney, and again Jimmy was there as a selector and entered for the Championship. In the first round he played T. B. C.
Hoey and beat him by one hole (see Recollections, p. 158). The
second round is well described by Vincent Mathers in the *Irish
Press* of Thursday, 27 June:

> The legendary Jimmy Bruen was cheered to an echo at Killarney
> yesterday when he won one of the most dramatic matches of his
> long career by beating Billy Ferguson of Malone in the second
> round of the Irish Amateur Close Championship to reach the last
> eight. Bruen who had beaten another Northerner, Brien Hoey, in
> the first round, even stole the spotlight from Joe Carr in this grip-
> ping encounter with Ferguson in the afternoon. The climax to this
> second round match was by far and away one of the most exciting
> seen on this course for many years, and what joy it brought to the
> Corkman's supporters.
>
> Bruen had seen a two-hole lead slip away from him when he
> lost the tenth, eleventh and twelfth to go 1 down. From that point
> the match took a dramatic turn. Bruen squared the match at the
> thirteenth, but then went 1 down again where he fluffed a chip shot
> [at the fourteenth] ... However, he squared the match again at the
> seventeenth where he played a shot that will be spoken about for a
> long time with Ferguson lying short in 2. Bruen was on the shore
> but played a magnificent shot to within 2 feet of the pin to snatch a
> win, when Ferguson missed from 6 feet. At the last hole Bruen had
> another escape. He put his tee shot to this famed short hole on the
> road and halved the hole when his opponent three-putted, and the
> end came at the first tie-hole where Ferguson put his second shot
> in a bunker and took 2 to get out.

With Bruen in the last eight were Joe Carr, Norman Baker, Paddy
O'Sullivan, Bertie Wilson, Eric O'Brien, Fergus Gallagher and
John Nestor. In the quarter-final Jimmy beat Fergus Gallagher of
Co. Louth by 5 and 4 and then in the semi-final match met Joe
Carr. Paul McWeeney reported on the match in *The Irish Times:*

> All that could ever have been dreamed about came true in the epic
> battle between those two great personalities of world amateur golf,
> Carr and Bruen ... [Bruen] has now proved himself one of the all-
> time masters and to have forced Carr to the very limit without hav-
> ing competed in any championship for seventeen years was an
> almost incredible performance.
>
> The standard of play in an atmosphere of electric tension was

extraordinarily high ...

... the strain of combat was absolutely intense. For sheer drama of the fighting qualities of both men this match will never be forgotten by many of the big gallery that followed it. It is worthy of note too that the best ball was 65, 10 better than par and between them they had an eagle and seven birdies.

In brief the story was of early dominance by Carr who set out in a mood of ruthless determination to prove that he could get the better of this wizard of the past – no matter how friendly they may be off the course. After eight holes Carr was 3 up with his score up to then of one under 4s. Then Bruen who had looked incapable of stemming the tide, struck his first blow with a birdie 3 at the ninth and suddenly the whole situation changed. He got another back at the short eleventh and squared at the twelfth. He saved his neck with his putter at the thirteenth, fell behind again at the fourteenth and snatched another improbable half at the fifteenth but could do nothing about Carr's eagle 3 with a 10-yards putt at the sixteenth, and so that was dormie 2 and, apparently, the end.

But the greatest thrills were still to come for the seventeenth. Carr pushed out his wedge shot on to the beach and could not get out so Bruen's sound 4 kept the issue alive and with that very difficult par 3 eighteenth to come, both must have felt that the rhodo-dendron bushes on the left and the lake on the right were closing in on them for they hit the nerviest of tee shots. Bruen's skimmed along just above the ground to finish in thick rough just off the shore and Carr's also was well short and almost under a tree. Bruen hit a superb chip to 4 feet from the stick and then Carr, under the most grinding pressure, produced one of the greatest shots of his illus-trious career. His perfectly struck chip rolled up to finish less than 2 feet from the hole and Bruen walked forward and shook his opponent's hand ...

I will always remember that day. It was one of those beautiful days in Killarney when the sun was out and the flowers were in bloom, and the course was in beautiful condition. What a stage for possibly two of the greatest amateurs to step on to the first tee. Although these two men were great friends, Joe, who was at the peak of his career at the time, did not fancy being beaten by anybody, and particularly by Jimmy Bruen who could have been described as making one of his rare emergences from retirement. My abiding memories will always be of the putting of James Bruen who saved himself time and time again with uncanny accuracy on the greens; of the wry smile on Joe Carr's face as putt after putt was going into the hole; and, finally, of the almost sentimental moment when, on the picturesque last green, the two players having played two wonderful recovery chips, Jimmy Bruen decided that he had had enough and shook Joe warmly by the hand. There was no question of asking Joe to hole the 2-foot putt to go into the final of the Championship.

There is one other nice passage in the *Cork Examiner's* report of that match:

> Thus ended a great match, one which will live forever in the hearts of those privileged to watch it and one which will go down in the annals of Irish golf. It evoked a warm tribute from twice champion Carr: 'I wish they could get him to retire properly because he is too good', and it brought a simple comment from Bruen, the maestro who came back to challenge for the Close Championship after more than 25 years and very nearly brought it off: 'I thoroughly enjoyed it and the better golfer won'.

That was to be the end of the playing career of the great James Bruen, and on what a fitting note it all ended.

17

THE BRUEN LOOP

If Jimmy Bruen had not had the famous 'loop' in his back swing, it is fair to say that he would then have been described as probably one of the most orthodox swingers of his day in golf. Because this loop was so unusual and unique to himself his swing was the subject of much discussion and conjecture, and many thousands of words have been written about that famous loop. Let us start at the beginning, however. Jimmy's grip was the orthodox Harry Vardon overlapping grip. His left hand was played at the perfect position with most of the back of his hand facing towards the hole, and he always used a left-hand glove. His right hand fell into place naturally on the club and if there was anything unorthodox about his grip it was the way that this right hand used to ride a little higher on the club than most players. He had, of course, immensely strong hands and always believed that a good strong grip of the club was absolutely essential. It was noticeable too that his right thumb always rested on the left hand side of the shaft of the club.

He favoured a completely square stance similar to that of Henry Cotton himself, except for the fact that Jimmy used to turn both his toes inwards. For the full shots, his stance was more on the wide side than the narrow side and he usually stood with his feet about the width of his shoulders apart. He addressed the ball with bent knees and relaxed arms. He always seemed to give the impression that he was digging his feet into the ground, while he usually took two short waggles before he started his back swing. At this point he would move his head to the right, seeming to watch the ball with his left eye, and in one movement from shoulders, arms and hands he would start the club back inside the line but very much along the ground for 2 or 3 feet. It was noticeable at this stage too that his hands were almost behind the club head. When the club got as far as hip level no player had straighter arms, and the club appeared to be as far away from the ball as was physically possible and more inside the line of flight than most players, and from here he went into what has been described so often as the famous 'Bruen Loop'.

From this point on in his swing his right arm appeared to bend and move even further inside, and his right elbow would stray right out from his body getting the club into a position which was nearly directly out over his head. From that peculiar position the club head did a circular movement inwards – whence the hands moved down very quickly towards the ball with the left hand almost leading the right in a sort of a whiplash action which undoubtedly was the source of his tremendous power.

When Jimmy's hands arrived at the ball, he was in the classical position for hitting a golf ball, head behind the ball, left hand leading the right and a perfectly balanced stance. It is interesting to note that throughout this most peculiar and unusual backswing Jimmy's head never moved – in other words, there was never a semblance of a sway in his swing. From here on he hit the club head at tremendous speed through the ball in a perfectly orthodox manner, finishing up with his hands high over his left shoulder and a braced left side, and the right hip following through after the club. This loop in Bruen's swing has been described by many people in different ways. I rather like a description by Robert Browning, writing in his newspaper of 17 October 1950:

> We have had champions before who had conspicuous 'loops' at the top of their swings, Massey and Bobby Jones are two of the most famous examples.
>
> In their case the 'loop' is due to some super factor such as a tightening of the grip at the moment of starting the club down, but in Bruen's case the loop is more of a flourish like the flourish a ringmaster might indulge in as a preliminary to cracking his whip....
>
> He is a powerfully built chap, and much of his enormous strength comes from the 'crack of the whip' which he imparts with his wrists and hands as the club comes through the ball.

Henry Cotton's 1938 description of the 'Bruen Loop' has been given in chapter four above. Even the great Bernard Darwin wrote a special article on the famous swing. The article, under the heading 'Looping', appeared, I believe, in *Country Life*:

> Whenever a golfer having something novel and noteworthy in his method greatly distinguishes himself, he has a rush of slavish copyists who believe that here is the secret for which they have

long been searching. This is no new development; it is doubtless as
old as golf itself....

... Bruen has a style entirely his own which is productive of
the most tremendous results ... it defies analysis; still more, it defies
imitation....

A very famous professional who was watching play at Birkdale came in one day having found a peaceful part of the links
where he could put in a little practice. Somebody asked him what
he had been doing and he answered 'I have been looping', but it
was an answer not to be taken seriously. Bruen has unquestionably
a loop in his swing ... But what exactly is the form of it? The club
head is going so fast at the crucial moment (that is why he drives
so horribly far) that no one can see what it is doing. I am told that
even to the camera it produces a shapeless blur ...

He seems at some point in the upward swing to take the club
head inward, then to take it outwards and so, after forming his loop,
bring it down straight along the line on which he proposes to drive.
In fact his swing appears the converse of that inculcated by the doc-
trine of 'hitting from the inside out'. Clearly he cannot bring it from
the outside in or he could not drive as he does, but probably by
some optical illusion it looks as if he very nearly did.

There is too this added complication. What I have been trying
to describe is rather the way in which he swung when we first saw
him. Now he seems to begin by taking the club much further outwards from his body, so that presumably he must also at some
point take it much further inwards in order to accomplish his loop.
Something odd and unorthodox happens to the right elbow which
is apparently for a fraction of time high in the air and assuredly not
in a position where the books say it ought to be. But frankly, I give
it up; since I cannot make up my own mind as to precisely what
happens I cannot hope to describe it to anyone else. All I can be tol-
erably sure of is the result, which is staggering. If there is anyone
who hits the ball harder or further I have not seen him.

Perhaps the only conclusion is that arrived at by the two gentle-
men to whom I listened as they refreshed themselves at the bar. Unfortunately their remarks must lose some of their pungency in print
since they must be interspersed with discreet and anaemic blanks:
'— the — regulation. I'll play my own — game. That's what he says
and — well right too,' exclaimed one of them and the other heartily and blankly concurred. I can add nothing to their wisdom save
that anybody who tries to copy the champion will probably break
his wrist and elbow and miss the globe into the bargain. 'Genius'
wrote Samuel Butler, 'might be described as a supreme capacity for
getting its possessors into trouble'. In this case genius is much more

likely to get his imitators into trouble and they are not likely to get
out again by hitting the ball 170 yards or so with a mashie niblick.

Frank Burke in an issue of *Irish Golf* magazine wrote:

> His swing is regarded as 'unorthodox' on account of a curious
> twirling action of his club at the beginning of his down swing. By
> way of apology for this I will quote Henry Cotton who said of
> Bruen '... Either his swing was wrong and all the others right, or, it
> might be that his was the swing and all the others wrong'.

In a series of extracts in *The Irish Times* from *Masters of Golf*, Pat
Ward Thomas, golf correspondent in the *Guardian* wrote:

> Of all the golfers I have watched down the years there was one
> whose name had a quality of excitement that was incomparable.
> Hogan and Cotton could stir the imagination and commanded
> attention by virtue of their presence alone. Thompson and Snead
> could create an awareness of beauty and all the other great ones in
> their different ways made a powerful demand on the senses; but
> the golf of none of these men had a greater dramatic appeal for me
> than that of James Bruen, citizen of Cork.
>
> Although few of the present growing generation saw him play
> and many indeed may scarcely have heard of him, those that did
> could never forget the image of his swing, surely the strangest that
> modern first-class golf has known, remains clear in my mind to this
> day. There can never have been a swing quite like it. He drew the
> club back inside the line of flight and turned his wrists inwards to
> such an extent that the top of the swing of the club head would be
> pointing in the direction of the tee box. It was then whipped, no
> other word describes the action, inside and down into the hitting
> area with a terrible force. There was, therefore, in his swing a fan-
> tastic loop defying all the canons of orthodoxy which claim that the
> back and down swing should as near as possible follow the same
> arc. There must have been a foot or more between Bruen's arcs ...
> The action of his hands was identical to that of wielding a whip,
> and one has but to try this to realise how much greater is the accel-
> eration into the hitting area, whether it be with a whip, a club or
> throwing a ball ...
>
> I certainly do not recommend anyone to loop deliberately in
> the quest for power ... with Bruen it was [necessary] and wisely at
> the time no one attempted to change his style ... To what extent if
> any his swing was responsible for the injury to his wrist that has
> hastened his departure from the tournament play, can never be
> known. Bruen denies that golf had anything to do with it. Soon

after winning the Amateur Championship in 1946 he was lifting a tile in his garden when he felt the sudden pain. Thereafter it was always liable to be troublesome, and none of the expert advice he sought nor treatment could cure it. Whatever the cause there was no doubt that the wrist had to withstand a considerable shock every time he hit a full shot, such was the force of impact.

In March 1970 Henry Cotton wrote in an article on the Jimmy Bruen swing in *Golf Illustrated*:

When he disappeared from the major golfing scene after the war after damaging the right hand, moving some furniture, there was a story around that he was faking because his golf game had slipped. But knowing him and his game well, I knew that he just could not hit the ball as freely as he had always done, without suffering great pain and it was this dread of hurting himself too much which handicapped him.

I have not seen Nicklaus hit better tee shots than 'young Jimmy' produced from his very upright arc; in fact, his driver head, when he first came into the limelight finished almost over the ball, at the top of the back swing. Nicklaus, a hitter in the same league as Jimmy, has the most upright swing in golf today and it is unusual to see the club shaft flying so near the head at the top of the back swing. Nicklaus, however, gets his two arms almost straight at head-high level of the back swing, a position I have never been able to copy ...

The flail or whip has been a sort of Bruen trademark – an impossible action for many to copy, but many golfers would do better looking for a bit of flail action in their swings instead of so-called square action and edge in a stiffer push ...

... I suggested to Jimmy a flatter arc might be worth a try, but after all these years swinging upright, even a slight alteration would feel odd ...

In my opinion, Jimmy Bruen's iron play was probably the most consistent part of his game. He used the same method as with a wooden club except that he advanced the hands a little bit at the address and slightly hooded the club face, otherwise his swing was much the same. With all clubs he normally hit the ball high in the air, although if he wanted to he could also hit them low, as I have seen him do on many occasions in windy conditions.

Over the years I don't think I have seen anybody as good from 150 yards to the flag as Jimmy was, and that includes professionals and amateurs alike. The number of times he got down in 2 from anywhere from 150 yards into the flag was quite astounding. When it came to using a pitching iron or the modern wedge, he was simply out on his own. He could play them shut faced, with hands advanced low, or he could cut them up in the air with an open face and stop them stone dead right to the flag. On many occasions I have seen the ball hop back a foot or two off the pitch mark, particularly in wintry conditions or on a seaside course.

Years ago when we were both young we used to practise this shot often together for many hours and it was what he taught me that made me into a useful pitcher with a wedge. He used to do another trick in practice as well, in the winter. He used to plug a number of balls by pushing them into the ground with his foot and then hit them onto the green. I once counted the number of times he got down in 2 with twelve balls from a distance of about 30 yards – nine times out of twelve.

So much has been written about the great Bruen method and the famous shots he hit, I often feel that many people have forgotten how good a putter he was. Here again his method was very personal. He putted with his toes turned in in a sort of pigeon-toed manner with a very firm left wrist and orthodox grip, but his left elbow always stuck out in the direction of the hole. Over the years his consistency over the putting green was incredible and while he did occasionally miss a short putt it was really his long putts and hole out putts from 6 to 10 yards that were so staggering. With every putt he went for the hole and expected to hole them out.

In later years when his wrist trouble meant that the rest of his game had deteriorated somewhat by comparison with his form when at his best, his putting always remained as good as ever.

Anyone who has seen Jimmy play golf would realise that he hit the ball prodigious distances. I am not saying that he was the longest player in the world but he was certainly one of them. No doubt there are examples of this enormous hitting all over Ireland and the British Isles on the various courses on which he has played. His two shots to the middle of the green at the fourteenth green in Birkdale at the final of the Amateur Championship in 1946 are now legendary. In an issue of *Country Life* of

January 1953 there is an interesting comment on Bruen's length:

> ... at least among his fellow amateurs there can surely be no doubt
> about his being the longest of his day. When the International match-
> es were played in Portmarnock in 1949 the drives of the players
> from all four countries were carefully measured at the ninth hole.
> The book gives Bruen's longest as 280 yards; second to him came J.
> B. Carr with 265, then two more Irishmen at 250, whereas none of
> the players of the other three countries could apparently beat 235.
> 280 yards is really a prodigious distance. Heaven knows Joe Carr is
> long enough; yet he was 15 yards behind, and all the rest compar-
> atively nowhere.

Needless to say, he had many fantastic feats on his own course
in Cork Golf Club. The twelfth hole which he used to drive regularly with a No. 3 wood is 313 yards long. One day I was playing with him and, at this hole, with a 3 wood, his ball pitched
straight into the hole but unfortunately stayed out of it and
stayed on the lip, cutting a big pitch mark into the side of the hole.
I have often thought that this would have been a very long hole
in one indeed if it had come off. He had driven the sixteenth
green, 320 yards long, and at least on one occasion been over that
green off the tee. And on the eighteenth, playing in a mixed foursome one day with Miss Pat Blake, he hit a prodigious second
shot out of a sand bunker with a 4-iron. I have paced that myself
and it is 237 paces to the middle of the green. Jimmy that day
actually hit a 4 iron out of the sand into the middle of the green.

18

CONNIE GRIFFIN

From the time when he was a small boy Jimmy had what might be termed his own special caddy in Cork Golf Club. In Cork golfing circles the name of Connie Griffin is nearly as renowned as that of Jimmy Bruen. Connie was much more than a caddy to Jimmy – it is fair to say that 'mentor and friend', would also be true – and I suspect that his influence on the Bruen golf swing was more than many would think.

Connie, a quiet spoken, kindly Irishman, was a gentleman to his finger tips. Though he was a shy man, only a few questions to him on golf in general or Jimmy Bruen in particular were needed in order to discover a wealth of interesting knowledge. Throughout all the years, I don't think I can remember seeing anyone else caddy for Jimmy at Cork Golf Club. As well as that, they used to spend hours together on the practice ground – it seemed that no matter how many practice shots Jimmy hit, Connie was there to collect the balls, often into the dusk in the evening.

In his younger days Connie himself was a fine golfer – he modestly claimed that he could play off +2, and this was confirmed to me by many of the older club members who knew him well. He was a sufficiently good player to prompt a number of club members to join forces to get him an appointment as a club professional in England in 1929. They also gave him his fare. However, when he got as far as Dublin, he couldn't find his passport – he discovered later that it had, in fact, been stolen from him. After that he came home. Although he was subsequently offered another job in America some years later, he decided that he would not try going professional again. He told me that he continued to play golf until 1939.

Connie had many recollections of Jimmy. One of the earliest was of the two of them watching a final of the Cork Scratch Cup in which J. D. MacCormack was a contestant. Jimmy was a schoolboy in short trousers at the time. Apparently at the fourth hole J. D. pulled his drive into heavy rough. When young Jimmy saw him take out a wood and against the wind at this par 4, he said to Connie, 'He'll never get it out with a wooden club'. J. D., however, hit a huge shot onto the green, and for years after when Jimmy, caddied by Connie, played that fourth hole, Jimmy would refer to J. D.'s shot as being one of the greatest he had ever seen.

According to Connie, in the late 1930s a Colonel Maybe was a regular visitor to Cork from England and was a very keen golfer. During his holiday in Cork he would go down to the club and look for someone to play with him – and if he could find nobody he would then go alone. On this particular day, he arrived on the first tee and said to Connie, 'Who is that young fellow over there? Do you think he would play with me?' Connie replied that he thought he would. The colonel sent Connie over to ask. Typically, Jimmy was delighted to play with the visiting colonel.

They met on the first tee and as the 10-handicap colonel was teeing up his ball he turned to Jimmy and said, 'By the way, have you got any handicap?'

'Oh,' said Bruen, 'I have.'

'What is it?' asked the colonel.

'+3,' replied Bruen.

The visitor was a bit taken aback and asked, 'Who are you?'

'I'm Jimmy Bruen,' was the reply.

'Oh God, I'm going straight home,' said the colonel.

Nevertheless, he was persuaded to play. According to Connie, he got his strokes off his handicap and got the biggest beating he had ever got in his life. He was beaten 8 and 6. Jimmy, to the great delight of the colonel, had gone round the course in 64, which for him was a comparatively normal occurrence. It transpired that when the colonel went home to England he happened to tell his story to a friend who was a journalist with a local newspaper, not thinking that his friend would use it. But there it was on the front page along with his photograph the next morning.

I asked Connie could he remember the lowest round Jimmy had done on the Cork course. He could not remember the date but was quite sure of the figures. Jimmy was round in 61. He remembered well that, going to the thirteenth hole, Jimmy was speculating whether he could break 60 or not. His figures for that round compared with the par of the course were:

PAR: 4, 5, 4, 4, 5, 4, 3, 4, 3 = 36. 4, 5, 4, 3, 4, 4, 4, 4, 4, = 36. Total 72.
BRUEN: 3, 4, 4, 4, 3, 3, 3, 3, 2 = 29. 3, 4, 3, 3, 4, 4, 3, 4, 4, = 32. Total 61.

Connie recalled an incredible shot played by Jimmy at the sixteenth hole. This hole is 319 yards long and the second shot is played up onto a high plateau green. On this occasion, Jimmy, from the tee, hit the ball over the pin and it pitched 10 yards over the green and stayed in its plug mark. Connie admitted that he had the wind behind him (it would be impossible for any human being to reach this green against the wind) but it was not a very strong wind.

At the 456-yard eleventh hole on another day, playing with Redmond Simcox, he hooked a huge drive into the rough where the ball plugged. Taking a No. 7 iron out of the 'plug', he hit the ball high into the air, an achievement in itself. 'Where is that?' Redmond asked Connie.

'Would you believe,' Connie replied, 'it's in the middle of the green!'

The twelfth is a 313-yard drive and pitch hole, uphill all the way – this green he used to regularly drive. In later years, Connie was caddying for one of our more revered senior members, Dr Paddy Kiely, who was, like everyone in the club, a great fan of Jimmy Bruen. He was held up on the tee for a few minutes and got talking of old times to Connie. 'This reminds me of Jimmy Bruen,' said Dr Pat. 'On 7 May 1942 [he even knew the exact date] there was a stiff breeze blowing against us at this hole'. Dr Pat said to Jimmy, 'I want to see you drive the green'. Taking a new ball out of paper, he 'had a go'. The ball pitched on a grass bank behind the green and rolled back onto the back edge, whereupon he proceeded to hole a long putt all the way down the slope of the green for a 2.

Many years ago, Jimmy played a match in the final of a club match-play competition against Jim Malone from Dublin who was then 6 handicap and who subsequently won the Irish Close Championship. Malone at the time was working in Cork and joined Cork Golf Club. Connie told the story: 'At the time Malone was playing great golf, and Jimmy said to me going out, "I'll never beat this fellow today".'

'Well,' said Connie, 'you'll have to play good golf giving him five shots'. Eventually Bruen was 3 down and four to go. The last four holes are all par 4s and he had to concede a shot to Malone at the seventeenth. Malone finished in 4, 4, 5, 4, which, owing to his shot at the seventeenth, was a net 4, 4, 4, 4.

'At the fifteenth,' said Connie, 'we saw Bruen's ball finish 6 inches from the hole in 2, so he won that, we came to the sixteenth – his second was 2 feet from the hole for another 3; at the seventeenth he was 6 feet from the hole and he holed the putt; and at the eighteenth he was 2 feet from the hole again – four perfect 3s and so Jimmy won 1 up'.

I asked Connie what they used to chat about when they were out on the practice ground. 'Well', he replied, 'I used to hear about good golfers in England and Scotland from time to time and I used to ask him when he came back from his trips were there any good players there. "Well there are many," said Jimmy on one particular occasion, "but there is a young fellow from America called Frank Stranahan, you'll hear about him in a couple of years time." And so we did. Jimmy always knew who was going to be good'.

I asked had Jimmy ever asked him to go to the championships with him. 'Once in 1939 for the Amateur Championship,' Connie replied, 'so I said to him, "What the hell would I want to be over there for? Sure you can beat the whole lot of 'em put together." He just laughed saying, "I'm glad your hopeful". And, of course, he knew I wouldn't go and did not ask me again'.

Connie told me that on another occasion two Corkmen from Douglas Golf Club went to St Andrew's where they had never been and they asked for two old St Andrew's caddies. On the way round they were talking a lot about various golfers when they asked one of the caddies who he thought was the best golfer, professional or amateur, that he ever saw in his life. 'There's a simple answer to that,' said the caddy. 'A young lad from Co. Cork called Jimmy Bruen, did you ever hear of him?'

'I live quite near him,' was the reply.

'Well,' said the caddy, 'we'll never see anything like Bruen again'.

Connie recalled a day when 'Mr Arthur Dinan, a well-known member of the club, called me over. He happened to have been over in America and in the hotel where he was staying he happened to meet Jimmy McHale the American Walker Cup player. They talked a lot about golf and in the end Mr Dinan asked Mr McHale who was the best player he ever saw, "I would mention two," said Mr McHale. "One is Jack Nicklaus and the other is Jimmy Bruen and they were much alike."'

I tried to find out from Connie if he influenced Jimmy's swing or method of hitting a golf ball and his answer was that 'Nobody could teach him anything about golf'. But he did tell me that, a few days before he went to Birkdale in 1946, Jimmy came down to the club for a lesson with Jack Higgins, the club professional. Jack was not available so he went to the practice ground with Connie. According to Connie, 'He was hitting the ball hopelessly, especially his iron shots … I left him alone for a good while and in the end I could see what was wrong and I told him that he was not getting away his left side at all'. So Connie made him have a few swings. 'Now,' said Connie, 'hit the ball like that', and apparently he hit a beauty. 'You're dead right,' said Jimmy, 'I have it now'. And of course Jimmy went off and won the British Amateur. 'Sure,' said Connie, 'it was only a small thing but I could see it and he could not'.

One day Jimmy was playing with a well-known player, S. H. McCarthy, better known to his friends as 'Spot' McCarthy. Spot could play golf either right-handed or left-handed and I remember he claimed a scratch handicap left-handed and a 3 handicap right-handed – I don't think that claim can be substantiated but he certainly used to carry a few right-handed clubs among an otherwise left-handed set of clubs and you never quite knew if you didn't know him well, which way he would play the next shot. Spot also had a great sense of humour and was always up to practical jokes. On the day in question, however, they were playing the second hole, a 477-yard par 5 in a friendly game. Jimmy hooked his tee shot into the rough and they were looking for his ball for a while, but obviously in the wrong place. Spot walked on further, found the ball and, by way of a joke, put his heel on it and plugged it.

'Oh come here,' said Spot, 'I have it – it's sitting up.'

Jimmy went over, suspecting that Spot was up to some trick, and said, 'It's sitting up all right, Spot.'

'Well,' said Spot with a smile, 'surely be to God even the great Jimmy Bruen can't put that on the green.'

'No trouble at all,' said Jimmy. The shot, according to Connie, was about 160 yards and Jimmy pitched the ball into the middle of the green.

'Now, Spot,' said Jimmy, 'what do you think about that? You thought you had caught me by putting your heel on the ball, but that was the only answer for you.'

Spot appreciated that the joke was turned back on him but he was mesmerised by the shot and said to Connie afterwards, 'I knew he would get it out reasonably well, but I never dreamt he could put it on the green – I didn't think that anyone could hit a ball that distance out of a plug mark'.

Connie felt that it was playing such devastating shots that damaged Jimmy's wrist. In his opinion, the worst thing that happened to him was just before the war when he was about 15 stone and lost 3½ stone on the advice of some English professionals.

Connie claimed never to have seen anybody as good as Jimmy to get out of trouble, or with approach shots to the green, and he felt that Jimmy was in a class on his own with long putts and chips from around the green. 'He expected to hole all these and was quite disappointed if he did not do so'.

For many years, when visitors came to play golf in Cork Golf Club from Great Britain, America and other parts of the world, they would ask: 'How good was Jimmy Bruen?' Those lucky enough to meet his old friend and caddy would get one answer from Connie Griffin: 'He was the greatest.'

19

Jimmy Bruen – The Man

What sort of a man was Jimmy Bruen? There is no doubt, to my mind, that he was gentle, kind, self-effacing, extremely shy, a moderate man, a family man, a fine sportsman, good humoured and, in my opinion, a reluctant hero. Yet he had plenty of inner self confidence, great integrity and determination, along with an ability for hard work.

When examining the personality of Jimmy Bruen in relation to the game of golf, I believe we have to divide it into two phases. Firstly, the pre-1940 Bruen and, secondly, the post-1945 Bruen. This, I believe, is necessary because it often happens that the boy may not be the same as the man. In the case of Jimmy Bruen, the inevitable changes wrought by maturity prompted a change in his outlook, indeed in his whole attitude to golf.

By 1939, although still but a schoolboy, he had already climbed the steep and difficult ladder of fame, had gone through pressures and experiences that most golfers of international standard would experience only seldom in an entire golfing career. And very few indeed would have reached the same or similar heights. One wonders how many schoolboys, put in the same circumstances as Jimmy Bruen, would have had the strength of character not to have emerged as rather too cocky, boastful overbearing youths.

Such was the case, however, with the 'Boy Bruen'. Inevitably, he was accused of being cocky – there are always those around who are jealous, or want to pull any successful individual off their perch. It is a tribute to Bruen that that was the only bad thing they could find to say about him. I believe that some people mistook the word 'cocky' for 'confident' – he was full of confidence. Without that confidence he would never have achieved what he did. Otherwise he was a rather shy man and, as a result of this shyness, tended not to be the life and soul of the party. He was, and indeed always remained, a rather self-effacing individual who would more often be found on his own, inevitably hitting golf shots, rather than taking part in what might be described as the more usual group activities of the average school-boy. His manners were always impeccable, above all in the company of his elders, the vast majority of whom admired him greatly, not only for his golfing ability, but also for his quiet, pleasant, unassuming manner. Henry Cotton described him as 'unusually level-headed for his age, but still a modest boy at heart'.

As a sportsman on the golf course I don't believe that anyone could criticise him. Winning or losing, Jimmy was the same, there was no bragging, there was no ill-temper and there were no excuses – if he had any strong feelings, as he must have had from time to time, he kept them to himself. I have discussed many people with him over the years and never once could I say that he was unkind or critical of anybody. I always felt that if he did not like someone or other he just did not discuss them at all. In his rather shy way Jimmy liked people and people liked him.

As a young man Jimmy was desperately keen on the game and anything to do with it – I think it was his whole life then – he never missed a chance to play with anyone anywhere. He strove to improve his game through practice or watching others play, having lessons, or reading books – anything that would help.

Nobody who has had the privilege of watching this incredible rather plump young man, with key chain always in his right hand pocket (a fashion in those days), hitting golf balls huge distances and going around all kinds of courses in record scores, can ever forget that thrill. The sheer power and strength, the inevitable loop, the loud crack off the ball, and, with an iron shot, the huge divots – all are sensations and aspects of the indelible picture that young Jimmy left on the minds of so many thousands of followers and friends. There seemed to be no heights which this boy could not attain in the game he loved.

Then came the war in 1939 and for Jimmy a serious illness and a long lay-off from championship golf. In 1946, when big golf resumed, there was no longer the carefree 'Boy Bruen' but instead this rather intense, busy, more mature grown man with many responsibilities to his family and his business, but who could still do extraordinary things with a golf ball. He developed horizons other than golf – he took a huge interest in his family and his house and garden, he took up sailing, he was very keen on shooting and fishing and became accomplished at all these other sports. He developed from nothing his business as an insurance broker and worked very hard at it. I believe that he really enjoyed seeing his business grow and gave it a great deal of his time.

In this second phase of the Bruen career, golf was no longer the all-encompassing driving interest that it had been, and somewhere along the line about this time he lost some of the competitive urge for 'big time' golf. It was, of course, his privilege as an amateur to do what suited himself. But such is the penalty of fame that the followers of the game wished and expected to see more of him.

He became a controversial figure and played only in the odd championship or representative team. There was much speculation as to why he was a reluctant competitor – I have heard many theories ranging from the idea that he might have lost his nerve, become afraid of the opposition, to the idea that it might even have been his wife Nell's fault. The latter is absolutely groundless as I know that on many occasions she tried to encourage him to play. But Jimmy was not easily persuaded by anybody – when he made up his own mind about something, that was really that.

What then was the real reason? I don't suppose we will ever know. It can be said that it certainly was not fear of the opposition – he proved that when he did play. Did he lose his golf nerve? It is possible but I don't really think so, for I feel that it would have shown up in his putting, and that touch never left him until the day he died. I personally think that he lost his enthusiasm, not for the game but for the limelight – I am sure that there was always a touch of the reluctant hero about him. The damaged wrist did not help when it happened, and maybe he used it as an excuse at times, but I feel that there was evidence of this lack of enthusiasm well before that happened. I wonder if he ceased to enjoy the battle. He was quite the opposite of Joe Carr, for example, for whom the more the battle raged, the more he enjoyed it.

Nor was Jimmy 'one of the boys' on the golf circuit, though he was most pleasant company and everyone liked him and he was welcome with any group of golfers that I ever knew. I was involved in many levels of golf then, as a player, selector and so on, and everywhere I went, I heard the same questions: 'How is Jimmy?'; 'Is he playing any golf?'; 'How's the wrist?'; 'We'd love to see him out again'; 'Is he playing as well as ever?'

Golf was good to Jimmy and many felt that he had an oblig-
ation to the public to turn out. Although that is a theory to which
I do not subscribe in the amateur ranks of any game, I am often
surprised how many of the post-war generation of golfers have
never seen him play! What a treat they have missed.

A charming article written in *Golfing* in August 1964 by Peter
Alliss I think demonstrates what I mean. He wrote:

> All my life (or at least most of the parts I can remember) the name
> of Jimmy Bruen has been something of a mystery. When I was four-
> teen or fifteen and spending many hours looking through the
> pages of record books, his name always seemed to be there ...
> Unfortunately I never saw him play, as indeed I never saw my
> father (by this I mean under tournament conditions).
>
> I first met Jimmy a few years ago when he was on a visit to
> Parkstone, where he had some relative living. That was really the
> only time, until May of this year, that we have ever met.
>
> I tried to find out what I could about him; how old was he?
> How did he injure his wrist? ... I discovered he was only in his
> early forties; rather like Bobby Locke, they both seem to have been
> with us for so long that one assumes they are much older. Also I
> was surprised to find so many conflicting reports about his prow-
> ess and his temperament ...
>
> ... John Jacobs was telling me Bruen went to see him at Sandy
> Lodge during the awful winter of 1962/1963 and that he stood for
> an hour and a half and hit balls as well as any amateur in Britain ...
>
> When we played the Jeyes Tournament at the Little Island
> (Cork) Golf Club last May, I had a chance to meet him, talk with
> and generally sum-up in my own meagre way, the man himself.
>
> I met him at the club. He walked a few holes with us. 'Are you
> playing, Jim?' they kept asking, some with knowing grins on their
> faces as if they knew the answer and reasons already. 'No, the old
> wrist has finally gone,' he said.
>
> At a cocktail party later that week in Jimmy's house I asked
> him about his game and how he remembered it. He told me he
> always went for the flag, and that he hit the ball 10 miles up in the
> air, 2 irons or 9 irons ... I found Bruen to be a modest man, with a
> lovely family, a beautiful home overlooking the castle at Blackrock,
> just outside Cork, a man proud of his past feats, and who consid-
> ered his best golf was played in 1946 when he won the British
> Amateur Championship at Birkdale. He told me he flew the mound
> on the left-side of the first fairway every round and only had a 6 or
> 7 iron to the green each time. What a tremendous advantage that
> must have been.

I admired his cups and trophies (he and Joe Carr must have all the silver in Ireland). Also the most delightful paintings which adorned the walls of the lounge and were signed Bruen. His mother had painted them he told me....

I asked him about the wrist and how it happened. 'Lifting crazy-paving stones,' he told me. 'When we moved into this house during the war it had no path round the lawn, so I set about making one. I lifted a large piece of stone and threw it into the wheelbarrow. I felt a twinge, thought no more about it, but it soon began to swell and set solid. From then on I have had everything done I can think of, copper bracelets, faith healers, cortisone injections, manipulations, quacks, the lot. Now it's full of arthritis and all the bones have set together in one block. I'm afraid I've had it'.

How sad, I thought. Here was a man who loved to compete, whose putting touch was still uncanny, whose nerve was still strong, put out of action by a bit of paving stone. Jimmy, I'm sorry I never saw you play at your peak, but I have asked and listened and read all about you. I am a fan, although maybe a distant one, but if I had three golfing wishes I think one of them would be used to put that old wrist right, and the clock back ten years so that I and many thousands of your fans could see you winning championships in a manner beyond belief.

James Bruen, golfer extraordinary and true gentleman, I salute you.

What a gracious and deserved tribute from another great player.

In May 1972 Jimmy Bruen died of a heart attack, five days short of his fifty-second birthday. He had been captain of Cork Golf Club twice and was president of the club the year he died. Unfortunately for him and everyone else he was not spared to complete his term – he was doing a great job for the club, especially with the greens, and was enjoying it thoroughly.

On 18 May 1972 in *Golf Illustrated* his close friend and mentor, Henry Cotton, wrote an article entitled 'Goodbye Jimmy', and I suspect that there may have been more than an odd tear in his eye as he wrote:

I never thought I should have to do a story on the late James O'Grady Bruen (Jimmy to us all) for this charming fifty-one-year-old Irishman died in the first days of May in Cork, where he had lived most of his exciting and full life. I loved Jimmy from the very first days I met an enthusiastic boy wonder, then aged eighteen years, at the Walker Cup matches at St Andrew's in 1938 ...

… From that meeting onwards we were great friends … Just a bare month ago, he and Nell, his wife, and mother of six children, spent three weeks in my home at Penina, and to have anyone in one's home for three weeks is a test of friendship, but we were genuinely sorry when they left. I wish he had stayed, he might still have been alive.

Jimmy built up a very successful insurance business in Cork, a type of business which always depends on personal service, reliability and a sense of responsibility, and he excelled at his job, but I am afraid at a damaging price to his health. He became president of his local club last year, an honour he appreciated as much as his Walker Cup team victory in 1938 and his Open Amateur Championship win in 1946, but it was extra work he could not do without a strain alas. He came to us for a rest, and was planning to live part of his future in the sun with us here, when he had eased off in his business, for he realised too late it turned out, he was 'doing too much'.

In his last letter to me dated 24 April – just nine days before he died – he talked of needing rain to help his greens at Little Island. 'Knowing our climate, I feel certain rain will come -- the Good Lord never leaves us short,' he wrote. He was a boy prodigy, winning all the junior events available to him, at the same time as he was winning most senior events he entered … I knew he was great …

… He had what I call a typical Irish face, rugged but attractive, and he enjoyed his life whether he was caravaning, fishing, shooting, sailing, gardening or golfing with his Nell, a youth-time sweetheart, whom he married when in his early twenties, his great love!

… So it is goodbye Jimmy, and I offer this little inadequate tribute to a splendid fellow, who left a blank in the lives of many folks outside his lovely family.

… I don't think I will ever forget him in action in his glorious youthful golfing days. His golf career at the top was short but it was exciting, very exciting.

At the time of his death which for so many, myself included, was a time of deep sadness and deep emotion – he was after all not only our club's greatest player, he was also our president and friend – I wrote an appreciation in my newspaper. On rereading what I wrote then I find that time in no way has changed my thoughts of Jimmy. It is an inadequate tribute but the best I can do.

It has been said before and will be said again that whenever the names of the world's greatest golfers are discussed the name of

Jimmy Bruen will be among them; there will be in the future thousands of words written about James Bruen, the golfing legend, and that is only just. He was indeed one of the really greats. However, there was far more to James Bruen the man, than being a great golfer. To those of us who have known him since he was a young man, there will always be a picture in our minds of a rather shy, somewhat retiring man, who bore the great burden of fame heaped on him from a very young age, with a humility that was striking. Few indeed would have had reason to boast of his achievements as he had, but that was not for him, in fact rather the opposite, he changed the subject with a gentle smile when his feats were being discussed. That Jimmy was a kind and gracious man has been many times demonstrated both on and off the golf course – he was not a man who criticised others. I never heard him do so; no opponent that he ever played with in the game he loved, could say that he had not played with the perfect sportsman and gentleman, whoever won the match, and of course nine times out of ten he won. He was as gracious a loser as he was a winner.

At times, because of his greatness, he was the subject of controversy, but Jimmy never got personally involved – golf to him was always put in the right perspective and always came after the more important things of life such as his family and his personal life. He believed that there were other things around him to be enjoyed; he loved nature, he was proud of his house and garden, he was a top-class shot, he played table tennis, snooker and was excellent at them all. At one stage he took to sailing successfully and no doubt was partly instrumental in his son's success in that field, of which he was justly proud.

By whatever standards success in this life is measured, James Bruen was a successful man; he ran a successful business, had a legion of friends, and of course in the field of sport, golf in particular, he was one so gifted that his extraordinary success was inevitable. This makes his death at such a young age a tragedy, firstly for his wife Nell and his family, for his friends, the community and the world of sport. I have had the pleasure of being associated with him in business and in sport and have known him as a friend for many years. For me at any rate, and I am sure for thousands of others, it has been a great honour.

POSTSCRIPT

RECOLLECTIONS
CONCERNING
JIMMY BRUEN

As a member of the 1938 United States Walker Cup team, I played in the British Amateur at Troon the week prior to the Walker Cup competition. Here, good fortune came my way because I was lucky enough to win this championship.

Then our team went on to St Andrew's for the matches, and the press was full of how well the British and Irish team was practising and was being led by outstanding scores from an eighteen-year-old golfer named Jimmy Bruen of Cork. I noted that he had not played in the Amateur Championship the week before, preferring to give himself more time to practise at St Andrew's because obviously his main goal was to win this cup for his team.

When Francis Ouimet, our captain, announced the order of his players, I was surprised that I was to play the number one position. I felt that day in and day out there were better players on our team than I. Then Captain John Beck told his rotation and I found I would play against Jimmy whom we had already nicknamed, 'Bruen the Bear'. I very much wanted to win our match because naturally without the 'Bear' in the amateur field, many would say I hadn't played the very best.

I recall that I was around in 70 in the morning round of our match and 3 up. Fortunately, my putts dropped from time to time during the afternoon round so I was able to hang on and eventually won at the seventeenth, the famous road hole.

I knew then that it was just a question of time before Jimmy would emerge as one of the great amateurs of all time. I think back to the career of my fellow Atlantan, Bob Jones, who played seven years – from age fourteen to twenty-one – without winning a single major title. These were called his 'seven lean years' and then the last seven were his 'fat years' because he won thirteen major championships in that period of time. I recall that in

1925, as a youngster of twelve years, I spoke to Bob at the East Lake Golf Club just a few days after he had lost the US Open Championship by one stroke. I told him I was sorry he lost. His reply was, 'Don't worry about it, son, you never really know who your friends are until you lose'. Then Bob, like Jimmy, went on to win many championships.

Going back to 1938, the British team played wonderfully well and, for the first time ever, came away with the Walker Cup. At the presentation ceremony, there was obviously such joy in the faces of the large gallery that Gordon Peters and I sang that great Harry Lauder ballad, 'Wee Dorch and Doris'. We were so proud when a high percentage of those present joined in with us.

Here in the spring of 1993, as I close in on my eightieth birthday, I think back over my golfing years and realise that the friends made along the way are far more important than victories or defeats. I'm proud that one of my friends was 'Bruen the Bear'.

CHARLIE YATES

There were those of us who lived in the Bruen era, and some were lucky enough to have played golf with him, I was one of those.

I played golf with Jimmy approximately 40 times in Portmarnock in his heyday. I believed in the years 1939, 1940 and 1941 and maybe a little later, that he was one of the world's six greatest players, Amateur or Pro.

It goes without saying, playing with Jimmy always left me short of money. He won the British Amateur Championship in Birkdale in 1946 and I felt if the war had not intervened he would have won the championship two or three times, and possibly a British Open Championship as well.

He and I were team-mates in 1949 in the Walker Cup at Winged Foot, New York and in 1951 in Birkdale. At this stage he was having great trouble with his wrist, but nevertheless no one liked to play against him.

My greatest memory of Jimmy was his magnificent short game, but best of all was his unbelievable recovery shots. The game lost a very great player and a great gentleman.

JOE CARR

I first met Jimmy in the late 1950s when we played a match against one another at Cork Golf Club. Kieran Allen, a scratch player from Ballybunion, and I played Jimmy and John Fitzgibbon, an International at the time. This was a match organised between Junior Interprovincial and Senior players in those days, I remember we halved the match.

I had heard so much about Jimmy Bruen, as his reputation was enormous in golfing circles in Ireland and throughout the British Isles. Jimmy helped me to get my first job in Pro-Golf at Royal Birkdale in 1961 and later with Henry Cotton at Temple Golf Club in London. I took up my appointment as Club Professional at Killarney Golf and Fishing Club in 1967.

Jimmy was a regular visitor to the Golf Club on the shores of Loch Leane in those days. He would always come down from Cork in the early spring and used to stay on the course just behind the present 1st green on the Killeen Course. Jimmy used to book me on Saturday mornings for a two hour coaching session. He was a great practiser even in those times. I had studied a great deal about his famous swing from film which was taken in his prime. I really looked forward to working with him on his game then. He was an inspiration to be around and the few games we had together were just magic. My time with him gave me great enthusiasm for my own game. The famous Bruen loop and his mannerisms were very infectious.

The Bruen Swing: His assembly or address was perfect in both grip and posture. The swing off the ball involved a lot of lateral shift of the lower and mid section of the body. The arm movement was high and to the inside. Bruen's tremendous power came from the way he changed direction from back swing to down swing, here he moved his weight forward considerably into the left side, but while this shift was taking place he looped or curled or to put it another way he flailed the club behind him. This move helped him shallow the down swing but more importantly to create the whip that gave him so much power. Wonderful hands, a supple body, great mobility and flexibility epitomised his swing.

Many people thought of him as a prodigious hitter which he was. I would compare him to John Daly or Tiger Woods even with the equipment of those days. Can you imagine what he would have been like with modern day equipment. However what impressed me most about his game was his incredible touch on and around the greens. He was truly world class in this department.

Bruen was a very private person with a lot of presence about him. After all there was a reputation to protect. It took time to get to know him and as our friendship grew he became like a father figure to me. He used to say 'You only have one life to live so you better show your best front'.

His lovely wife Nell who later did great work for the ILGU and became president in the 1980s and his charming family where great to be around. His untimely death in his 50s was tragic for his family and for the game of golf which he loved. I personally miss him as a great friend and companion and when those spring days arrive in Killarney I am always mindful of him.

A truly great player, but also a fine gentleman.

TONY COVENEY

GOLF PROFESSIONAL TO KILLARNEY GOLF & FISHING CLUB SINCE 1967

The boy was a champion and the champion became a legend. He was, truly, a giant of the game whose individualism became a byword and whose fairway feats have become part of the game's folklore.

And he learned his golf in Muskerry, a course as tantalising as it is challenging. This is where the Bruen legend took root. Jimmy Bruen was not of the classic swing mould and anyone in Muskerry during the player's formative process would attest to that. The purists were amazed at his swing and, at the same time, in awe of his achievements. In the hills and dales of Muskerry, Jimmy Bruen found his sporting niche and he never looked back as he plundered the record books with results so formidable that he became a legend in his own lifetime. Renown wasn't confined to any defined theatre: the world became his stage and he played it with consummate application ... In the days that were in it, there was no provision at Cork Golf Club for boys to be accommodated with a handicap. So young Bruen made his official amateur debut at Muskerry. And so the story began. It continues today, not alone in Muskerry but wherever golf is played. I'm made conscious of this and the Jimmy Bruen legend in the many travels I'm obliged to make throughout Europe and elsewhere today. Jimmy Bruen belongs to golf.

We are fortunate that he honed his talents in Muskerry and we are very proud of that; proud that we provided the opportunities to play competitively and to demonstrate his genius. He represented Muskerry with distinction and at a level that no other has done before or since. He was a boy with us playing a man's game to such a degree of power and prowess that he was rightly dubbed a prodigy. Muskerry embraced Jimmy Bruen and he responded by giving so much in return. There was nothing triumphalist about the boy and those men of his era were always enchanted to personally enjoy the splendour of his golf and the awesome scope of his achievements. They were captivated by a swing that had no parallel: they were enthralled by a player who rewrote the record books at home and abroad. Muskerry gave him the space to accomplish all and that stands to the eternal credit of its members. Those who knew him and played with him respected his talents and encouraged his ambitions. He was always one of them but, because of his astonishing achievements, he was destined to become an international figure, a golfer with genuine world credentials. And we all shared in that in a meaningful and tangible way for Muskerry's reputation grew with the wonders of the boy and the reputation he cemented in the glorious triumphs of the man.

He was nothing less than a phenomenon. When he joined Muskerry as a rather portly youngster of 15, he started with a six handicap. Six months later he was scratch and before he was 18 he was a mind boggling plus six. At this prohibitive handicap for any mortal, Jimmy Bruen continued to win, taking the prestigious President's prize with 82 stableford points over 36 holes. The story of his feats are endless and golfers, a touch sensitive to listening to exploits other than their own, never tire hearing and recounting his deeds. That was the measure of the man, the boy who grew to stardom on Muskerry terrain, which gave him every opportunity to exploit his talents.

That is the way we, in Muskerry, remember Jimmy Bruen and that is why there is always reserved for him that exalted status in the club. His memory and his deeds will abide forever.

PATRICK J. FOLEY
PRESIDENT EUROPEAN GOLF ASSOCIATION

My memories of Jimmy Bruen are mostly local and in any case his National and International records are well documented. I think the first time I realised Jimmy Bruen's unique ability on a golf course was when he holed out in 29 strokes one Easter on the original 9 hole course in Parknasilla. He was, I think, playing with Dick Browne, then Chairman of the ESB and would have been about 14 or 15 years old.

I well remember an Open Stroke competition in Little Island played on a St Patrick's Day when he had a 63 gross and won with 67 nett, out in 30 and back in 33. Five fours followed by 3,2,3,2 for the first nine. I wonder has it ever been done since. Neither of us were married then and played and travelled locally many times. We played in and won a fourball in Killarney for the 'Mid Summer Goblets' which Lord Castlerosse had presented to the club. He, Castlerosse, was a good friend of Jimmy's and a great admirer of him. That day I reckon Jimmy had eleven pars and seven birdies and this off the back tees in the original Mahony's Point. There are other stories like this such as the time, in a match, when he had two pars and seven birdies on the first nine holes in Muskerry.

The outstanding memory for me was, however, seeing Jimmy in the Irish Open Championship going around the Royal County Down links in Newcastle in 66 shots. Sixty years or so on I think this record still stands.

DICK LORD
CORK GOLF CLUB

My first memories of the late Jimmy Bruen were of reading about him in the *Cork Examiner*. His swing with the famous 'Loop' seemed to fascinate everyone. The marvellous scores he returned even when playing against the professionals in the 'British Open' impressed everybody, even though golf in those days, 1936/38, was an 'old man's game' and here was a teenager showing everyone how it should be played at its best.

Everyone spoke of his colossal length off the tee and the divots he took with his iron shots.

Needless to say I was thrilled in the 1950s when he invited me to play with him at Cork Golf Club.

All the above accolades were correct but what stands out in my memory was his accuracy from 100 yards to the green –

always landing 6/8 feet from the hole, and I honestly believe he was one of the best putters I have ever played against.

Jimmy was not only a wonderful golfer, but also a quite unassuming person, who loved giving encouragement to any youngster.

TOM EGAN
MONKSTOWN GOLF CLUB

My first meeting with Jimmy Bruen was in the dining-room at Knock Golf Club. Jimmy had played with W. S. (Billy) McMullen and I with the redoubtable Joseph B. Carr. The year, confirmed by Joe, was 1937. In the course of conversation I mentioned that there was a Semi-Open Fourball *v* Bogey at Sutton the following Saturday and both Jimmy and Billy accepted our invitation to play. Although only 15 years young both Joe Carr and I were senior members of Sutton paying then an annual subscription of £3.3.0. per year *[see photograph]*.

On telling my father of our invitation he thought it wise to inform the Golf Club that the latest up and coming star in Irish Golf would be playing on the following Saturday evening. All hell broke loose – the committee felt that if Jimmy played on Saturday evening there would be no entries for the competition as all members would be out watching instead of playing. By agreement Joe and I absented ourselves from school that Saturday morning and had a wonderful morning's golf. Jimmy off +4 and 17 years old was my partner whilst Joe Carr partnered Billy McMullen of Knock Golf Club and also 15 years old. The result of our efforts on the day was that Jimmy and I had 12 up whilst Joe and Billy had 11 up. I can recall our Hon. Sec. James A. Doyle writing down Jimmy's address for the purpose of sending him the first prize of a 3 guinea voucher. Low and behold that evening then medical student one Harry Counihan and Sutton's Dan Cotty returned a 13 up to win on the day. Jimmy however received his envelope containing the runner's up prize of a voucher for one guinea.

An interesting score was made at the 4 par 7th that day. With plenty of run on the ball Jimmy played a 4 iron on to the narrow green. Joe a three iron with Billy and I playing drivers and all balls made base. Billy and I two putted for 3's whilst, of course, the two stars of the future each holed for 2's. A total of 10 for the hole. By the way someone at Sutton decided to inform the press of Jimmy's visit to the club hence the photograph a copy of which I am sending herewith. The appearances of this photo in a newspaper made hash of our proposed illness excuse to our schools on Monday.

During my two years in Cork 1940 to 1942, when apprenticed to the shoe trade at the then Central Boot Stores on the Grand Parade under Jack Cunningham, I spent many Wednesday evenings – our half-day – practising with Jimmy at Muskerry. I was also a member of the winning Muskerry team which won the Cork Winter League in those two years. The team was led by Jimmy followed by Dr Billy O'Sullivan and Eddie O'Flynn. I was next followed by Matty (The Prince) Murphy, Dr Pat (Archie) O'Connell and Michael (Mick) Hegarty.

Not only was Jimmy a good customer of mine in Grafton Street when he needed to be shod but also a very good friend. I am sorry he left us so early in life.

MICHAEL FITZPATRICK
SUTTON

I never had the pleasure of playing a full round with Jimmy Bruen. What can be said about the man, that has not already been said? Many years ago in Galway, my good friend Jack O'Donnell, and Larry McCarthy, told me stories of the great Jimmy Bruen – this man with the loop in his back-swing who hit the ball so far yet had a touch of velvet around the greens.

They talk about the 'Big Bertha' today – years ago Fred Smyth made woods at Royal Dublin for Jimmy Bruen, with big heads, very similar to the 'Big Bertha'. One could only imagine how far Jimmy would hit his driver, with the shaft of today. One story I heard, which is well-known – Jimmy in short pants was taken by his mother to the Championship. She asked the Pro Mr Halsall to play a round of golf with Jimmy before the start. As the Pro was very busy he just took Jimmy to the practice ground for a few minutes. He then told Jimmy to hit his drive. The reply was 'if I hit my driver Mr Halsall I will hit it over the boundary' – 270 odd yards. Having seen the drive then hit, Halsall played nine holes with Jimmy and knew straight away here is material for a world-beater in the boy. He then got on the phone to the bookies and placed a 'fiver' – a lot of money in those days for a win. Believe it or not the great Jimmy came to me at Royal Dublin for a lesson – his wrist was causing him trouble at the time. Then I saw the greatness in his 'grip', the way the club fitted into his hands, how I would have loved to play 18 holes with him.

CHRISTY O'CONNOR, SNR

When I came into Championship golf in the early 1950s I was fortunate enough to encounter some of the great Irish golf legends of the 1930s and 1940s who were approaching the end of their playing careers. Among those I played with were J. C. Brown, Cecil Ewing, Dr Billy O'Sullivan, Willie Meherg, but one man stood out like a beacon, and he was the late Jimmy Bruen.

Jimmy had unaccountabaly disappeared from the game in the early 1950s when he was still a young man, so when he came to the 'Amateur' at Royal Portrush in 1960, his encounter with an English undergraduate player was literally 'the only game in town'. Jimmy was four up playing the fourteenth hole (Calamity) and gave his opponent the match, apparently due to a sore hand. Nevertheless we had witnessed flashes of great genius, and I was glad to have seen him with my own eyes.

You can imagine my trepidation and delight when three years later I was drawn to play him in the first round of the Close Championship at Killarney. Jimmy and his charming wife Nell had a caravan behind the old fourth green by the lakeside and he was persuaded he should enter the Championship – thank goodness.

I was fortunate enough to enjoy a career in golf that lasted another twenty odd years, and it is fair to say I never had a greater thrill than the day I played Jimmy Bruen, even though he was but a shadow of his former self. What an utterly charming man he was – will we ever see his like again?

BRIAN HOEY
BELFAST